# CONSERVATION OF TEXTILES, BONE AND IVORY

# CONSERVATION OF TEXTILES, BONE AND IVORY

A.S. BISHT

AGAM

AGAM KALA PRAKASHAN

DELHI

First Published : 2010


ISBN : 978-81-7320-100-4



*Published by:*
**Dr. Agam Prasad,** *M.A. Ph.D., Diploma in Museology*
*for* **AGAM KALA PRAKASHAN**
34, Central Market,
Ashok Vihar, Delhi-110 052
Ph: 27212195, 47098550, 65688806-07
Fax: 91-11-27212195
E-mail: *agambooks@gmail.com, agambook@yahoo.com,*

*Type Setting by:*
***Amit Graphics***
*Delhi*

*Printed at:*
**Chawla Offset**
Wazirpur Village,
Ashok Vihar,
Delhi - 110 052

**DEDICATED**
**AT**
**HIS LOTUS FEET**

# PREFACE

Ever since the National Museum Institute (A deemed to be university) was created in the year 1989 this has been a milestone in the journey of Conservation in this part of world. The three faculties were created which were awarding M.A. degree in their respective disciplines e.g. History of Art, Museology and Art Conservation. It's products are doing commendable work of successfully helping the country in the tasks which they are involved so as to make available the personnel for attending to the needs of art works in the possession of various departments, governmental, private or otherwise in India and even in other countries of SARC or elsewhere. I thankfully acknowledge to the authorities having associated me as a Visiting Faculty Member to teach Art Conservation, even after my retirement from the post of Head of the Conservation of the National Museum, New Delhi. Accordingly, I have contributed my bit or so as to create adequate personnel to fulfill the commitments envisaged for the field of Conservation of cultural heritage.

As I look back in retrospect from 1958 onwards I have witnessed the establishment of its various departments, galleries and the projects undertaken by the National Museum, New Delhi. I consider it my good fortune, which of course has given me adequate impetus to venture in the publication of some books to help the students in order to pursue their studies in Museology in general and Conservation in particular. It is true that I have played an active part in the upsurge for the care and conservation of cultural property in India. There has been a general consciousness for the collective care/conservation by systematic management of museums & the importance for total safety of the collections while conducting the various activities in a museum starting from acquisition, documentation, conservation, storage, display, exhibitions, transportation and handling of the artifacts after the creation of the NMI.

One of my books in this series "Conservation of Wooden Objects" has been published by the NMI and now I am very happy to say that it is within my reach to prepare similar books specifically on various topics of Conservation though the NMI had interest in some other publications and I had to decide to get these published from private sources in a changed format of including two topics in one book like the present one. God willing and thanks to the NMI and my friends in profession of publication to see my dream come true. I am the only one still teaching under all the VC'S and remember them all on this occasion. I have used the slides and photographs of the artifacts belonging to the National Museum and I duly acknowledge their photo credits to them. A large number of these have been taken by me while I was Head of the Laboratory and are being used only now. I am grateful for the help rendered to me by the various departments of the NM and duly acknowledge this fact. I also take this opportunity to thank the present VC, NMI for support and the confidence in me. I would also like to thank all other colleagues at the NMI/NM for support especially (Dr.) Prof. K.K. Jain, Dean, Academic affairs & S.P. Singh, Director (Con.) who took over from me twenty years back. I have ignored the personal expectations of my family members while preparing this publication. God forgiving as I firmly believe that all works are God's work and I am grateful to the publishers of this book Dr. Agam Prasad of Agam Kala Prakashan, Ashok Vihar, Delhi-110052. and his staff. I also acknowledge the help given to me by all my colleagus all over India to keep me still useful for the profession for completing the publication in a minimum period of time.

A.S.B.

# CONTENTS

# LIST OF ILLUSTRATIONS

## Part I

### *Figures:*



### *Plates:*

# Prat II

## *Plates:*

# PART I

# CONSERVATION OF TEXTILES

## CHAPTER I

# INTRODUCTION

Stone age tribes learnt to sew skins together using needles made of bone. It is reported that the earliest material was leather known as applique work. The first farmers discovered how to extract linen thread from the flax plant, how to spin fleece of the sheep and weaving it into a fabric for clothing. The length wise threads warp on the loom over and under which is the weft threads are passed to make cloth. We wear cloths basically to keep us warm besides for the reasons of modesty. Some people feel it is to attract the opposite sex. The textile making, presumably must have been a home industry world over initially and it thus, had an extremely long and rich history. It, therefore, had an impact on the world economy and the evolution of modern society. Textiles though had a glorious past, our people especially the Crafts men have been taking pride in their achievements who made these fabrics for the elite of those days are in our possession and are as old as the respective civilizations. Yet it is also a hard fact that there are not many surviving examples of these today in India. The only exception is reported of fragments of madder dyed cotton, woven in coarse plain weaves which have been recovered from the excavations at Mohenjo-daro. This shows that the people of the Indus valley knew how to grow cotton, spin, dye and weave it to make a fabric. From it even at that point of time more than 5000 years back. Panini in the first millennium B.C. writes of cloths known by their colours. However, there are no records of the tools used by them or its evolution.

Rig Veda (V.55.6) an many other ancient texts reported to have mention Maruts wearing mantles adorned with gold which shows that art of weaving was known to Indians well before the advent of the Christian era. The murals at Ajanta and other contemporary cave sites like Bagh depict figures and figurines shown wearing beautiful dresses. Several stone sculptures from different parts of India, through the ages, are shown wrapped in fine and many a times, transparent dress symbolizing the dress worn by them. For example there are depiction of a transparent drapery in the sculptures of ancient Indian sites such as Gandhara (Plate 1), Sarnath and Mathura (Plate 2) in the North Amaravati and Nagarjunakonda, Sanchi and Barhut reliefs, and many other sites spreading through out the geographical boundaries of this great country of ours down the centuries. During the first three centuries of the Christian era materials from India especially the fine muslin cloth from Dacca now in Bangladesh and Tanda in Uttar Pradesh in India was sold in the markets of Rome at a very high price. We are anyhow are left with a very scanty evidence in the form of material products although the tradition speaks of a well developed textile industry, though it might have remained active in many colonies of Bunkars (Weavers) of those days, in India somehow or other and which is being supported by our government by giving financial grants to the Weavers to keep the art alive. Literary evidences in old texts, depiction in paintings, illustrated manuscripts and sculptures are the testaments of their existence especially in early medieval period. Buddhist literature is reported to have many references to the magnificent weavers of India in and around Kashi (Varanasi). A cotton cloth was provided to wrap the body of the great Buddha after He attained nirvana, eternal rest.

The textiles collection of the National Museum, New Delhi is magnificent as regards the traditional textiles of the later Mogul period. It is but natural that the most of the acquired textiles in it's collection do not go back than the Mogul period. On the other hand it possesses two very ancient textiles collections, some of them are still intact but most of them are in fragmentary state which have been collected by Sir Aurel Stein and party during their third trip to the Chinese Turkistan (1913-1916 AD) from two burial grounds particularly rich in textile finds from Lou-lan and Astana. Special mention can be made of some examples of polychrome figured silk as well as some monochrome figured silk which are superb from many aspects and are preserved in the Central Asian Collection (Plate 3) of the National Museum, New Delhi. Many of the coloured motifs look so fresh and familiar to Indian motifs. Kushan tribe who established an empire through Gandhara as far as the river holy Ganges, converted to Buddhism and thus opened a route for the religion to enter Central Asia and hence be carried to China.

During the early part of the 2nd cent. A.D. when the Kushan Empire reached its greatest heights under Kanishka, peace reigned from Rome to China and for more than two centuries commerce, art, and religion moved freely by land and by sea along the caravan trade highway known as the Silk Route. There was a well defined diffusion and intermingling of the two cultures between the fifth to ninth century A.D. as reported by Janet Harvey in the book "Traditional Textiles of Central Asia". The Textiles shown in the book have obviously a great similarity with the fragments of the Central Asian textiles in the National Museum, New Delhi as reported above any one can visualize that the past of these textiles must have also been glorious.

It also has a very important pre-Columbian art collection of ancient Coptic textiles (Plate 4) from South America which has been donated to the National Museum, New Delhi as part of it's Western and pre Columbian Art Gallery by one great collector of artifacts of Indian origin who had, settled in New York called Mr. Nasli Heeramaneck. According to late Dr. Grace Morey the first Director of the National Museum, New Delhi it is a superb collection in quality and in it's representativeness of the major indigenous cultures of America's from Mexico, south to Chile, Peru, Maya, Inca, north-west coast of America, Panama, Costa Rica and el Salvador. Ranging from about 800 BC to the Spanish conquests in the early part of the 16th century A.D. It is called 'pre-Columbian' because these artifacts mostly belonged to the period before Christopher Columbus unknowingly reached this part of the world in search of a new sea route to India in 1492 AD.

Leaving aside, the irony of fate that majority of the textiles in its collection, the National Museum, New Delhi today are from the Mogul period till the present times. In costumes especially belonging to India, color predominates with lavish splendor not only in the landscape but also in the vivid and fabulous costumes of its people. Indeed the people of India have a rich, exotic and varied tradition in cloths, chiefly due to its variety of climates, wide-spread geographical locations, diverse festivals, arts and crafts, social customs in the different parts of the country.

If we try to ponder the reason we, Conservators, do agree that it is difficult to maintain them especially in the tropical and sub tropical climatic regions of this part of the world. It is also true that besides their maintenance to keep them in good condition people did not realize that their decay process has to be well understood and that to in totality to save them. There are, therefore, many reasons for this and unless the subject is studied in detail it would not be possible to draw correct conclusions. However, we are left with very scanty evidence of ancient Indian textiles although the tradition speaks otherwise.

## 1. TECHNIQUE:-

In costumes especially belonging to India color predominates with lavish splendor not only in the landscape but also in the vivid costumes of its people. Indeed the people of India have a rich, exotic and varied tradition in cloths, chiefly due to its variety of climates, wide-spread geographical locations, diverse cultural ethos, festivals, arts and crafts and social customs of the different parts of the country. The designs of the clothes used indicate knowledge of ikat, patole techniques of tie-dyeing of yarn before weaving, of bandhana, tie-dye of cloth, as also indigo and manjitha process of painting and dyeing cloth, to create designs where colour forms a dimension, and outlines merge with a fluidity to form the pattern. A large number of references can be cited to this effect by the researches done by our scholars on the subject. I have touched only a tip of the iceberg since it has a definite need to pass it on to the Conservators of today. Textiles in India have been very colorful and are reported to be a major part of our exports even in the past.

We learn that a number of different fibers were being utilized for establishing these textile producing centers which were working on the basis of their highly developed technical skills which were being used by the Weavers of those days in India. Many accounts of travelers are available from different parts of the world such as Macro Polo and Chau Ju–kua to name a few. It has been reported that remains of Indian cloth have been found in Egyptian tombs and Japanese temples. Records also indicate that Ikat textiles were produced in India for the Arab world. The warp and weft are patterned in such a way that when woven, the dyed sections are aligned to form a single unified pattern. Some of the important centers of producing textiles in India were Bengal, Orissa, Malwa, Gujarat, Bharoch, Cambay, Multan (now in Pakistan), Mysore, Musulipattam, Kalahasti, Varanasi, Hyderabad and Assam to mention a few. The Indian Weaver expressed itself in cotton, silk and wool with the patronage of some enlightened rulers and the skill of migrating artisans. In the east the emphasis has been on texture, ornament and sophistication woven on cottons and silks. Double Ikat is reported to be done in a small village called Tenganan in the Island of Bali, Indonesia. Many countries claim to have been producing Ikat world over.

The entire textile collections can be divided into the following broad categories such as woolen, silken, cotton etc. which are further subdivided into two main categories i.e. plain and patterned. These could further be divided into four types. (a) Woven, dyed, embroidered and printed. (b) Zari Brocaded work (c) Carpets and Tapestries. (d) Costumes plain or patterned or with zari work (e) Decorated Flags, Fans and other decorative textile objects not covered in a, b, c, d above.

## 2. LOCATION OF TEXTILES:-

Out of a total of over 400 Museums in India about thirty or so have collection of textiles worth mentioning such as the National Museum, New Delhi, the Bharat Kala Bhavan, Varanasi; the Prince of Wales Museum of Western India, Mumbai, the Indian Museum, Kolkata, the Salarjung Museum, Hyderabad, the State Museum, Lucknow, the Museum and Picture Gallery, Varodara, the Government Museum and Picture Gallery, Chandigarh and the last but not the least the only museum in India which is solely devoted to textiles namely the Calico Museum of Textiles at Ahmedabad of which we know has specimens of different fabrics, woven, printed and embroidered in India from the 15th century. The exhibits include costumes actually worn by the noblemen: jamas, patkas and the angarakha; Mughal tent encampments and canopies of the 16th century, tapestries, wall hangings and other cloth accessories. In the east the emphasis has been on texture, ornament and sophistication woven on cottons and silks. It is clear that textiles are very difficult to maintain once they start decaying or become weak. In fact their decay starts the moment these are made due to lack of proper knowledge or understanding the factors of their decay. The conservation of textiles is one of the most versatile branches of conservation. Besides these many museums, temples, royal palaces and private individuals also have old textiles with them. India is truly a colorful country and so are it's textiles. Besides this we do have many other examples of paintings on textile such as Kalamkari, pichhavaies and many more such examples on textile which are actually paintings on textiles drawn by a kalam(pen) and are to be hung in the temple at the back of the deities and hence the name. Many more examples of textiles such as Kantha, Thankha, Prayer mat, Floor spread, Wall hanging, Embroidersied Chamba Rumol (Plate 5) Jain Patas, Phadas of Rajasthan, Orissa Pata Chitra, Nepali Pata Chitra, etc. can be cited and have to be dealt as paintings, perhaps separately.

## 3. LITERARY EVIDENCES:-

The 'Yuttikalptaru' describes textiles of four types based on their source namely tree barks, silk, cotton and wool. The texts advises that in making cloth the threads of one type alone are to be used; mixture of threads renders the cloths inauspicious. It adds that according to the craftsmen there are many colors and shapes of silk cloth. 'Kauseya' being the term for Indian silk naturally finds frequent reference in the works of the period, indicating there by its common use. It would, therefore, appear quite natural that the term was sometimes used as the general name for silk. But as 'Medhatithi' clearly says it was a particular type of silk. The 'Yuttikalptarua' speaks of many varieties of cotton cloths according to their appearance, thinness and the like but without giving any details says that all these can be used by every body. The Yuktikalpataru describes lomaja cloth as made out of the hair of animals. These are of four types. Here also the texts repeat its advice of not mixing the different types of hair. Fabrics made of wool proper find mention in ancient literature such as the mention of the word kambala by north Indians including the Nepalese for a blanket. Similarly the use of the bark of many trees have been mentioned in the literatures on the subject. It speaks of three kinds of barks which have been used for the purpose namely from the trees grown in the forests, marshy land and ordinary lands. A mention of the bark of ksuma or linseed plant is available in some early Bengali literatures and in these texts.

One of the reasons for India's supremacy in the textile markets of the ancient world seems to have been the fact that she early developed and mastered the technique of preparing fast dyes from natural sources. In fact the use of dyes dates back to remote antiquity. Natural dyes were used throughout the centuries until the appearance of synthetic dyes in the mid 19th century. Even in the time of Panini and the Nikaya texts this appears to have been a developed art. On the analogy of the eight ragas of love in ancient Indian literature, we also have eight dyes namely the dye of safflower (kusumbha) which is reported to be permanent if protected, and is destroyed soon if not cared for, Vermillion (sindura) is dry in nature and sticks if used with oil, Saffron (kunkuma) is pleasant if used in small quantity but is unpleasant if used thick, Lac (laksa) canstick only when heated; when cool it does not stick, Madder (manjistha) is lasting and can survive long use if it is first heated and then cooled down, the reddish brown dye called kasaya lasts when dry but is destroyed when mixed with oil, the dye made of Turmeric (haridra) vanishes very soon even though protected and Indigo (nila) lasts even after the material is destroyed and remains unaffected even if removed. The various characteristics of these dyes have also been explained mentioning which dye is fast and which is fugitive. Turmeric(haridra) vanishes very soon even though protected and Indigo (nila) lasts even after the material is destroyed and remains unaffected even if removed. For coloring cloth the most popular dye appears to have been Safflower. The texts of this period also give us an idea of the preparation of the dyes in those days. Early dyeing theories and dyeing theories based on the latest research data are reported by (Peters 1964) reported that the origin of dyeing and theories of how the colouring material is held in the fibers. Dyeing theory dates from 1734 A.D. when helot proposed a porous fiber theory of dyeing. Solid solution and chemical combination and colloidal theories were advanced at early dates. Modern theory shows dyeing as a multi- stage process which involves chemical combinations and physical forces. Many aspects of dyeing including effects of salt and acids are discussed and a tie-up between the early and modern theories has been explained. The NRLC, Lucknow (B.V. Kharbade and O.P. Agrawal-1988) took 39 samples of textiles for the identification of natural dyes from the Calico Museum of Textiles, Ahmedabad, with a view of their study for substantiating the mention in ancient literature. The results have been published as mentioned in the bibliography.

It is needless to say that colored garments were much in vogue and they could even be re dyed if desired especially if they have faded. There are mentions when different colored garments were used in different seasons by Indians. This only proves of our developed tastes and colorful life taking full advantages of our multi seasonal climatic variety and natural surroundings. A mention of these colorful clothes with varied designs printed and embroideries has been made in a very famous publication 'Kadambari' and also in other references of those gone by days. The art of gold Embroidery on the other hand was fully in vogue from those early times as supported by some physical examples of such dresses in our collections in museums though not so old yet of a few centuries of history and mentioned in the Memoirs of the Archaeological Survey of India e.g. an early medieval painting from Nepal. Siva as wearing a silken cloth with 'hamsa' decorations. In the works of the period we get references to the processes and implements connected with the art of weaving. The high technical skill of the weaver is reflected in the fine fabrics which he could make. This type of cloth is appropriately represented by fluttering wavy lines on the sculpture figures of Pala and Sena periods. Our textile industry was, therefore, highly skilled well comparable to the industries in China and elsewhere. We had many centers of this industry spread over almost all parts of India, running throughout its length and breadth from west Bengal to Gujarat and Kashmir to Tamilnadu besides many other parts of the once undivided India.

## 4. MATERIAL OF TEXTILES:-

Textiles are of varied nature and are composed of different materials. The English word Textile has its origin from Latin word textiles from texere or weave or texture. They are, therefore, a type of cloth or woven fabric. Basically textiles are made by a process of weaving or are woven on a hand driven loom or machine operated loom. However, there are some other objects which are also kept in this category like the ones which are knitted by hand or otherwise. Normally, therefore, we are required to attend to textile conservation which is limited to the natural fibers of animal and plant origin: wool, hair, silk, cotton, flax, jute, hemp, nettle, grass etc.

The textile materials encountered most often in archaeological sites are linen, cotton, wool, and silk. Linen is a spun and woven vegetable-based fiber derived from flax stalks and branches. Linen fibers lie close together and are durable. Linen does not take dye well and is usually left in a bleached or unbleached white state. All textiles get deteriorated by light, insects, air pollution & microorganisms which, alone or together, cause considerable loss of tensile strength and pliability. The oxygen in the atmosphere affects all organic substances to varying degrees. Prolonged exposure to normal atmospheric conditions will cause textiles to weaken and disintegrate. The speed of the deterioration varies according to environment and the nature of the fibers. The main factors that promote the decay of textiles can be categorized into three groups. Most of the textile materials are made of fibers and having flexibility as its basic property are also called textiles. To understand their properties better we have to get acquainted with the nature, source and composition of its material for which we have to study and go into their material sciences.

Textile fibers are natural i.e. available in nature which have been used by man for its various needs from very early times. The natural fibers are short, except for silk which may emerge from the cocoon in unbroken filament. They are further divided into three categories namely of (i) Vegetable origin are cellulose under which come fibers of cotton, flax, jute, hemp and ramie (ii) Animal origin which encompass protein fibers of which wool and silk are made (iii) Mineral origin which are not fibers in the true sense and are made out of metals like gold, silver, brass, copper and their alloys in the form of threads or thin laminates by a process of passing them through a machine to be drawn into a form of wire or made into very thin laminates by a process of beating as is usually done in India since metals are malleable in character. This has also been studied by me while visiting the workshop of a Goldsmith along with late Prof. L. J. Majewski from the Conservation Center, New York while I was with them in 1983 under Indo-US cultural exchange program. Decorative textiles with metal (gold, silver and copper) embroidery threads have been used gloriously in our places of worship like temples, churches, etc. or by royalty or high nobility. According to Sir George Watt the earliest complete accounts of wire drawing may be said to have been written by the distinguished novelist Colonel Taylor, and he has been followed by many others later. The pure wire was called *Sona-Kala battun* and the inferior as *rasi Kalabattun*. When the wire is thick, it is known as *badla*. The gold, silver, sparkling metallic strips are largely used for decoration with gold and silver embroideries, and are called *sitaras*. The gold wire is twisted with silk thread over which turmeric has been applied so as to impart a better tonal effect and flexibility of the fiber. Use of metal threads with animal hair core, metal threads made of pertinacious substrates, gilded metal embroidery threads, zari the metallic thread as used in Indian textiles and extremely thin gold layers on gilded silver threads, including the modern threads were studied by various Researchers in detail by using simple microscopy as well as the Scanning Electron Microscopy have been reported in bibliography. These decorative dresses, contain metal decorations and their cleaning, conservation care and storage require careful consideration of these old objects, otherwise these may suffer irretrievable damage.

In order to chalk out a proper conservation treatment of these decorative artifacts it is very necessary to know their chemical composition and method of making, in order to enable the conservators to execute the best possible treatment according to their needs. The decorations consists of wires, coils, strips, spangles, coated membranes etc.. The strips are flat or wound(spun) around a core of fibers. Wear and contamination can make it difficult to judge with naked eye which metals are present, and chemical analysis and understanding of the technology of fabrication provides the answer.

Man made fibers are recent in origin as their discovery is not very old, They are (a) Synthetic (b) Regenerated (c) Transformed and (d) Inorganic. Cellulose fibers are of plant origin. Cotton, we get from a plant named Gossypium herbaceum which is grown in India, America and Peru whereas Linen is produced by the plant Linum usitatissimum which is grown in Russia, Belgium, Holland, England and Ireland. Wool from a sheep is called Merino, from a goat it is called Cashmere and from a rabbit it is called Angora. Silk on the other hand is produced by a silk worm called Bombex mori when it forms cocoons. Manmade fibers came into large demand after the growth of population, are either synthetic or chemical. Synthetic fibers are Polyesters, Nylon, Acrylic, Polyethylene, Polypropylene, Rayon, Regenerated fibers is viscose, Transformed fibers are Cellulose acetate and cellulose nitrate but Inorganic fibers are known as Fiber glass and asbestos but have not been used as textiles to be worn but for upholstery and furnishings.

CHAPTER II

# PHYSICAL STRUCTURE OF TEXTILES

**Cotton** plant has fruits or bolls which burst open into fluffy is the only unique cellular fiber in the family of vegetable fiber which with the exception of cotton are multi cellular. Cotton is a vegetable fiber derived from lint on the cotton seed. It can survive moderate alkaline conditions but is adversely affected by acids. Cotton does not transmit moisture like linen and is very absorbent in its processed state. It is this characteristic which allows cotton to take dyes well. Cotton has characteristic clockwise twist; for this reason, it is commonly spun in a 'Z' twist. The cell wall has three main layers that is the cuticle, the primary wall and the secondary wall. The center of the cell is hollow and this cavity is called lumen. The cuticle is composed of wax, pectin and

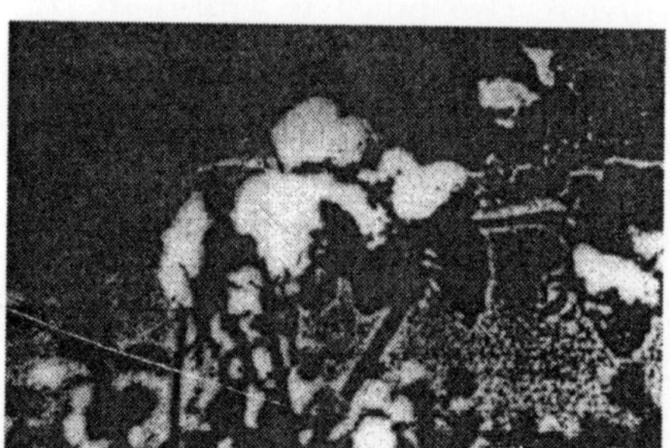

Fig. 1. Source of Cotton

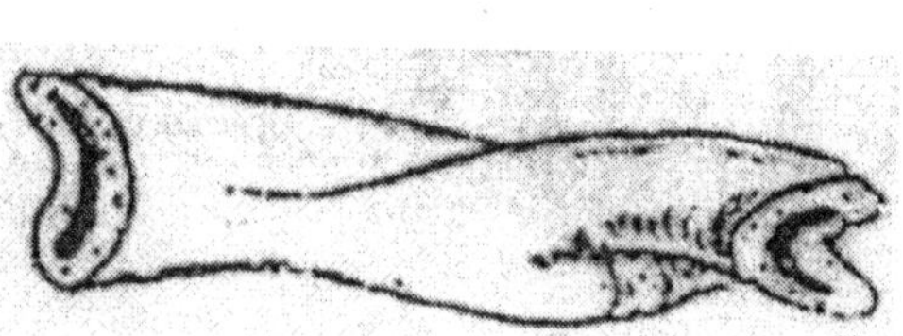

Fig. 2. Cotton Fiber longitudinal section

proteins that are removed in processing. The primary wall is about 0.1 mm thick consisting of three layers of fibrils each of different angle to the axis. The secondary wall is about 0.4mm thick and the fibrils in this wall are laid down in spiral formation 20-40 degree angle to the axis. It is the secondary wall that provides mechanical and tensile strength to the fabric. The center, as already mentioned, is hollow and is known as the lumen.

**Silk** is composed of Fibroin and sericin which are further made of amino acids. It is a natural protein and the animal fiber is produced by caterpillars belonging to the genus Bombax. Silk is an animal (insect) fiber that is derived from the cocoon filament of the silkworm. Because it is basically protein, silk is easily affected by alkalis and various inorganic acids. Like wool, it easily absorbs moisture and will take dyes readily. These dyes, however, are not as light-fast as those on wool. Silk is as strong as a steel wire of the same diameter but is very light sensitive. Therefore, it will break down faster than wool when exposed to ultra-violet rays. A single filament is the product of a series of stages derived from the cultivation of mulberry trees for feeding the propagation of the domesticated silk worm, Bombex mori. During the caterpillar phase, the worm wraps itself in a liquid protein secreted by two large glands in it's head. This secreted protein hardens upon exposure to the air. The resulting filament is bonded by second secretion, sericin, which forms a solid sheath or cocoon. Under natural conditions, a moth eventually breaks through the cocoon. In sericulture, the larva is killed in the cocoon by the steam or hot air in the chrysalis stage before its metamorphosis. Sustained heat processing softens the hardened sericin so that the filament can be unwound. The first continuous filament makes up into net silk that is usually made into fabric before it is relieved of gum in hot soapy water so that the filament can be unbound. The first continuous filament makes up into net silk that is usually made into fabric before it is relieved of gum. Special finishes and short lengths from the residue are weighing of the fabric is carried out & made into spun silk after removal of the gum for desired textiles. In the process of spinning, fibers are drawn out from a bulk supply and rotated at high speed twisting them to form a continuous thread or yarn. The twist can be given in many directions which could be loose or tight. Even several threads can be then twisted together to get the required form bulkier and stronger threads.

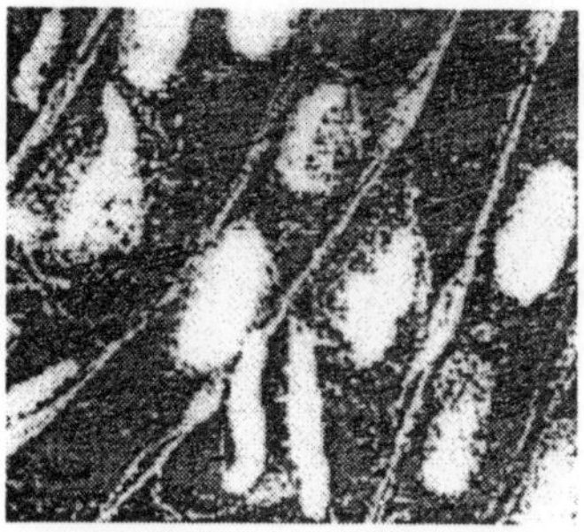

Fig. 3. Source cocoon-excreta of Silk Worm (Bombyx mori).

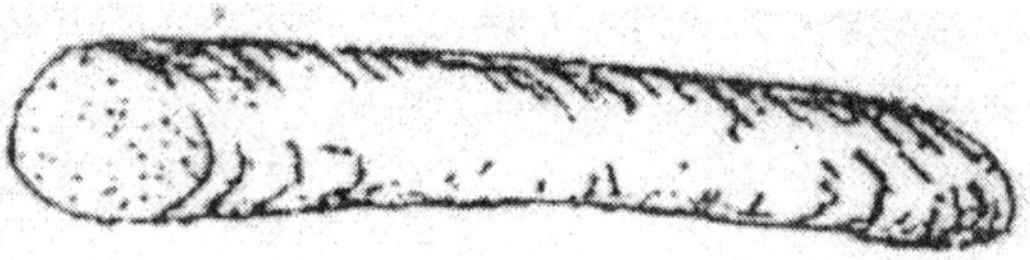

Fig.4. Silk Fiber longitudinal section.

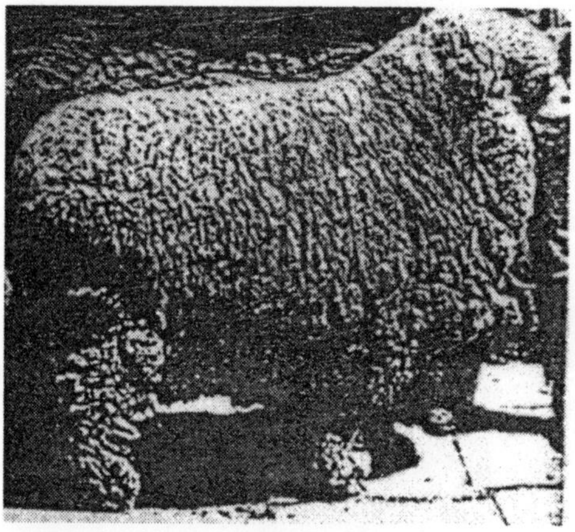

Fig.5. Source of Wool animal hairs

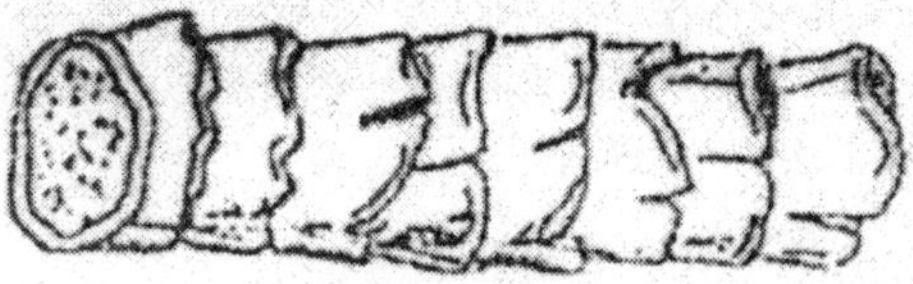


Fig.6. Wool Fiber-longitudinal section

**Wool** is basically composed of a special protein called keratin, which differs from others on account of its high sulphur content. Wool consists of protein fibers. The majority of the amino acids in the protein of the wool are keratin, which contains insect-attracting sulfur. Wool fibers absorb more moisture and accept dyes better than vegetable fibers. Wool is not a strong fiber and weakens considerably when wet. Raw wool from the fleece of a sheep/goat is cut off or sheared which however may contain 30% to 70% of impurities. The impurities are wool fat, dried perspiration, dirt, mineral matter and burrs which are dried vegetable matter. The textile chemistry shows that the strength of fibers and their consequent decay resistance especially when they age is directly related to the length of the molecular chains of which they are made. As a matter of fact when a textile decays, the internal bonds in the molecules are broken, making the chain shorter, leading to weakness, even to the breaking point of the yarn.

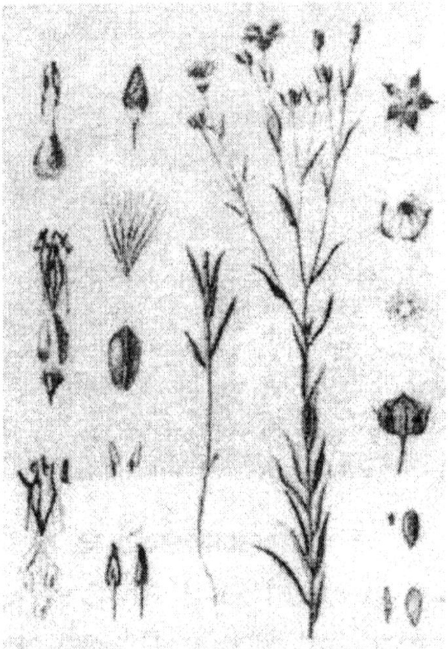

Fig.7. Source of Linen –Flax plant.

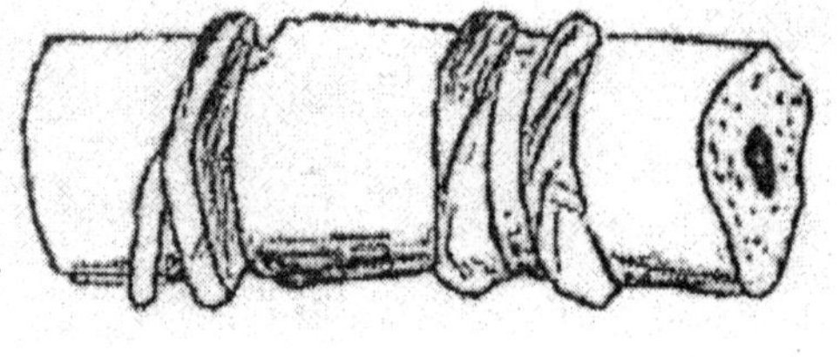

Fig.8. Linen Fiber-longitudinal section.

**Linen** comes from Flax. It is extracted from the fibrous bark of a plant belonging to the natural order linaceae, and the species is Linum usitatissimum. Flax plant is grown in Russia, Belgium, Holland, England and Ireland has also been used as a fiber for textiles especially the cánvas as a painting support. Linen is a bast fiber consisting of natural cellulose, and the fiber is obtained from the stalk of a plant mentioned above. It is uprooted in such a way as to obtain the maximum length of the fibers. The chemical composition of flax is very similar to cotton. Many products from this were being made like carry bags, shoes, hats and furnishings .When linen fibers have been wet they rotate as they dry in the direction of the center part of the letter S. It was noticed early that if such yarns are spun in this direction they would tighten or at least stay tight when washed. A linen canvas with single yarn Z spun, no matter how tight it is stretched to begin with, will continue to loosen in a damp climate. The Fiber structure and the sources of the four fibers mentioned above can be given the pictorial shapes as given above:-

## 1. CHEMICAL STRUCTURE OF TEXTILES

**Chemically Cotton is as follows:-**

Cellulose——85.5%, Oil and Wax————0.5%, Mineral matter—1%, Proteins, ketones and coloring matter——5.0%, Moisture ———8.0%

**Chemically silk is as follows:-**

Silk Gum or sericin——22-25%, Silk or fibroin——62.5 to 67%
Water—————— 10 to11 %, Salts——————.5 %-1%

**Wool chemically is as under:-**

Keratin ———33%, Dirt——————26%, Suint——28%
Fat——————12%, Mineral matter——1%

**The chemical structure of linen is as follows:-**

Cellulose———64.1%, Hemi cellulose—————16.7%,
Pectin—————1.8%, Lignin———————2%,

## 2. IDENTIFICATION OF TEXTILES

While identifying the textile samples we have to consider many aspects of the study such as the condition of the sample whether it is fragile, we have to take a minimum possible sample without any harm to the aesthetics and physical state of the textile as a whole for fiber analysis. Fibers that compose a fabric should be identified before any treatment is undertaken since the accurate identification of fibers is of importance particularly if stain removal is required. Due to the limitations at our disposal we have to restrict our study to the morphological features under various microscopic techniques over the normal measurements of the parameters e.g. solubility test, acid and alkali test, estimation of the moisture regain percentage and it's moisture content etc. which not only require bigger samples but are not related to it's identification. These parameters are important but due to our limitations of sufficient amount of the sample we skip them. The steps included in the technique of identification are as detailed below:-

1. Burning test.
2. Staining tests.
3. Study of the longitudinal section of the fibers under microscope in transmitted light.
4. Study of the above in dark field illumination.
5. Study of the transverse section of fiber under microscope.
6. Study of medulla in case of wool fibers.

Burning test is regarded as one of the reliable and authentic tests. Cellulosic fibers give the characteristic smell of burnt paper, they burn readily leaving only a small ash. The protein fiber burn irregularly leaving a black residue and gives a smell of burnt hair. Since wool and silk are protein containing they could be distinguished with chemical test. Physical tests, such as burning, quickly identify the presence of animal fibers, which do not burn readily and shrivel into a residue of carbon. These fibers usually emit the distinct odor of singed hair. Vegetal fibers burn easily to a fine ash. Many fibers and hairs can also be readily identified by microscopic examination. Animal hairs, for example, can be identified by their characteristic cuticle patterns and medullar cross sections. Simple staining tests enable the conservator to distinguish between the different kinds of fibers.

***Fiber Analysis-Micro-Chemical:***

| Material | Action of acid | Action of alkali | Action of Shirlastain A or C |
|---|---|---|---|
| **Wool** | No action | Readily affected | Stains Golden Yellow Dark/Green |
| **Silk** | Dissolves | Hot con. Dissolves | Stains dark brown or dark blue |
| **Cotton** | Readily affected | No action | Stains pale purple or Dull Pink |

A vital study in fiber analysis is to view the longitudinal section under the Microscope in transmitted light. The fiber is mounted in water or glycerin. All the possible morphological characteristics are studied preferably between 10x and 20x the joints or nodal points are well defined by the dark field illumination technique. Some surface structures e.g. the shape of fiber edges and striations, on wool though can be studied as well under transmitted light, but not as best as viewed under dark field illumination. We thus have a better view of the surface of the fibers by allowing the light to fall directly on the specimen. These two techniques further help in the classification of the seed and bast fibers on one end and different probable animal specie of wool on the other hand.

The conclusive study is conducted on the cross section of the fiber. The thin cross section of the fiber is viewed which reveals the pigment granules, the characteristic surface structure and shape of the fiber for confirmative identification. The thin section 100 microns or less is cut by a suitable microtome, which is then mounted on a glass slide with glycerin as mountant and viewed through the microscope. The cork and thread method has been found suitable for the purpose with a very low budget and has been described in my book (Scientific Aspects of Heritage Study -2004). Readers may like to refer to it. This work was initiated earlier with the active assistance of late H.K. Naithani when he was in the National Museum, New Delhi and later published as a joint article by us. The study of wool fibers does not end here and for it the study of the medulla is carried out. It is the central core of the hair which serves as food pipe for fiber when the animal is alive. The medulla in the fibers are seen continuous, intermittent, broad, double channeled or thin depending upon the grades and type of the wool fiber. It is generally missing in a fine variety of wool. The fibers are subjected to 17% potassium hydroxide solution in cold on a microscopic slide. The medulla develops in a few minutes. The technique is suitable for identification of all cellulose and silk fibers but it needs detailed practice to identify the wool fibers. If the specific animal species has to be pinpointed the morphological characters of the fibers of sheep-marino or ordinary sheep, cashmere or mohair or goat hairs, camel or alpaca or vecuma of llama hair (camel family) differs slightly leaving few exceptions of wool. It is further realized that my students will do further research after compilation of cross sections of known species to compare after collecting these from allover India and come to the definite conclusions. Infra-red spectroscopy can give a very quick and certain identification of minute samples of fibers. Each type of fiber has its own unique spectrum, and with modern equipments these spectra can be compared to the spectra of known fibers, stored in a computer.

I and late Naithani have done analysis of a number of textile samples in the laboratory of the National Museum in respect of its Central Asian collection and some samples from its textile collection.

All these results are published in the Journal Conservation of Cultural Property in its various issues cited in the bibliography. The results can be summarized as under:-

1. Acc. No. L.C. ii 016/65 sample No. 1 as Coarse Variety of Goat Hair.
2. Acc. No. L.C. ii 016/65 sample No.2 as Fine quality of sheep wool.
3. Acc. No. L.M.II ii N/M-678 sample No. 3 as fibers of mixed goat family (white) and fibers of mixed camel family(brown).
4. Acc.No. L. A.X. (07) sample No.4 as fibres of mixed variety of camel family.
5. Acc.No. L.C.vii. 01 (665) sample No.5A as fine quality of sheep wool.
6. Acc.No. L.C.vii. 01 (665) sample No.5B as fine and coarse wool fibers of goat family.
7. Acc.No.L.C.vii. 01 (665) sample no.5C as Ramie.

Krishna Riboud (1969-70) cited in the bibliography reported on the basis of analysis done in CRSIT, Lyon has reported about four fragments of textiles as under:-

(a) Acc. No. L.C. iii 04c (NM237) as a polychrome figured silk with woven inscription from Lou-lan.

(b)Acc. No. L.C. 02 (NM18) as a polychrome figured silk from Lou-lan site with both selvages present.

(c) Acc. No. L.C. ii.05b (NM173) as a monochrome patterned silk in "herringbone" twill weave from Lou-lan.

(d) Acc. No. L.C.vii.09 (NM150) as a monochrome Patterned silk (damask) from Lou-lan site.

The Conservation Laboratory of the National Museum also investigated the reasons for a peculiar phenomenon of decay of a Mughal Jamewar shawl of c.16th cent. from its collection, in which the warp and the weft were behaving differently. The warp was identified as domesticated silk and the weft was wool hair. Since the sericin of the silk was not completely washed at the time of its use it contributed in its decay but the wool was protected by its sulfur content. The Examination of Metal from Historic Indian Textiles in the National Museum, New Delhi, using Scanning Electron Microscopic-Energy depressive X-Ray Spectrometry was done and published by Prof. N. Indictor, a Professor of Chemistry, New York, when the former was on a AIIS grant in India in late eighties, and myself using Light Microscopy and the SEM facilities of the Metropolitan Museum of Art, Objects Conservation Laboratory, New York and the findings have been published in Conservation Of Cultural Property In India, Vol. XXII (1989) by the IASC and readers are advised to consult it for further study. Textile samples from a Velvet Palanquin cover Mughal, embroidered in golden threads (Acc. No. 48.7/108), 18th cent. AD, a Brocade *dupatta* woven with floral designs, Mughal, with silver and golden threads *sitara* work, (Acc. No. 60.1534), a Brocade *Odhani* woven with geometrical designs in golden threads (61.458), *Chanderi*, a *Maroon* Cotton Sari, printed and golden thread in between (Acc.62.1705), south India,19th cent. AD, a white cotton floor spreading having lining, embroidered in chain stitch with floral designs (Acc. No. 62.1777) and a yellow muslin brocade choga,Varanasi,19th cent. were studied by this method and results tabulated in the above referred Journal of IASC.

## 3. PROPERTIES OF TEXTILES:-

It is the property of textiles to age and weaken. Cotton and Linen are stable against strong alkalis but strong acids dissolves them. Dust and dirt promotes their decay. Soiling, ferruginous matters accelerate the formation of sulfuric acid, sulfur dioxide, oxygen and water, soot may contain sulfuric acid which decays cotton and silk, Hydrogen Sulfide would tarnish silver in metallic threads and *zari* yarns. Wool and silk dissolve in strong alkalis whereas wool is stable in strong acids but the silk gets dissolved in strong acids. Mechanical properties include tensile strength, tensile stress and strain, extensibility, elasticity, modulus and flexibility. Physical properties include shape, length, density, surface morphology. Chemical properties include oxidation, reaction to pH conditions and promoting bio-deterioration as these may act as culture for bacteria and fungi.

## 4. WATER IN TEXTILES:-

All natural fibers absorb and desorbs water vapor from the atmosphere unless they are already in equilibrium with the surrounding environment. It is, therefore, necessary to know the fiber's moisture sensitivity which can be measured as moisture content of a textile. It occurs at the surface and also in the amorphous regions of the fiber. The relative amounts of amorphous and crystalline material in the fiber are related to the fiber's capacity to hydrogen bond which would determine it's moisture sensitivity. Swelling and shrinking results in dimensional changes. In the beginning when the fiber is strong it can cope and adopt even the considerable changes but when it becomes old it can not cope with these changes due to changes of RH and later it can not adjust it self with these changes which results into decay. Too dry conditions make them rigid so as to reduce it's flexibility and the natural feel. Their elasticity is thus reduced in so far as it depends on the crossing the threads and the weave. Nevertheless, fibers retain a certain capacity to swell and contract. If the provision of maintaining the round the clock static conditions of RH etc. are there, it is the experience of the author also that it is difficult but not impossible to reduce the stress and strain on the fabric to take care of the fatigue in the fabric. It would also depend on it's manufacturing techniques, weave structure and it's patterns.

If the threads are closely knit the fabric would be much more durable than the loosely knit fabric and it's properties would get modified if it is knit with bulkier threads. In other words if the ply condition or number of threads being used at a point of time can be increased, the textile would be stronger and durable in composition. Moisture content of air dried linen is least, followed by cotton, wool and silk of their respective weights. When the same fibers are exposed to an atmosphere saturated with moisture, the linen absorbs least, followed by cotton, wool and silk in an ascending order. They have different affinity for moisture. Dampness is one of the major causes of damage to textiles, since these are quickly attacked by mould, fungus and start rotting.

## 5. METHOD OF MAKING A TEXTILE:-

Textiles as we see them at this point of time, we must realize that a lot of activities have gone since the fibers were gathered together and before we see them as a finished fabric. These activities have to be visualized to understand their nature and hence their conservation. A through understanding of the ancient textiles i.e. familiarity with their nature, historic and technical development is an essential for determining which of the measures for their long term preservation have to be taken., a diminishing fraction of what existed in the past are pieces of historical evidence which are more or less indispensable for research purposes. The ancient textiles still in existence, therefore, are very precious for any country to possess.

Weaving is believed to be one of the oldest surviving crafts in the world today, the actual origin of which is reported to date back to Neolithic times about 12000 yrs ago. Even before that time, the same principle was used to interface branches and twigs to form protective fences, shelters and baskets once the practicality of interlacing these kinds of materials was understood, further experimentation with other natural materials probably produced the first basic fabrics and cloths. Cotton yarns from India are Z-spun and they tighten with washing where as S-spun cotton yarns tend to pull apart. There are some basic habits of fibers. Wool and silk can not be made to move with moisture. Sheila Landi in the Textile Conservator's Manual mentions that there are three main weave structures namely (i) plain weave i.e. tabby (ii) diagonal weave or twill in which weave system based on a unit of three or more ends and three or more picks, in which the binding point moves along by one end at each pick, forming a diagonal line in the weave (iii) improved weave but similar to twill i.e. satin and from these three binding systems all others are derived. Besides this the metallic Zari has been used world over for decorated textiles especially in India by using innumerable different techniques.

It is also reported that the earliest textile fiber was made from wool of a sheep. It was first converted into fibers which were drawn into fine thread and were then twisted to form a long yarn on a spindle. Our early ancestors probably twisted a few fibers from a lock of wool to form an extending length of yarn which would be wound into a ball. At a later stage the yarn was wound on to a stick and a simple flywheel added at the lower end to produce a spindle. From this the spinning wheel developed, invented in India which was named *Charkha* and then reaching Europe in the late 14$^{th}$ century. It goes without saying that the textiles were woven earlier by using hand driven looms (Plate 6 & 7) till the textiles were woven by machine. For centuries the spinning and weaving both were traditionally continued by hand as a cottage industry. All family members were helping in the job. However, the textile fragments which are available today, speak of their glorious past achieved through these hand looms. At times one wonders how the so called crude looms could be used to get such skilled works of high quality which could be achieved by our ancestors. It is also reported that the early loom was as simple as a branch of a tree running parallel to the ground.

This reminds us of our crude looms being used by our tribal people even now in some remote corner of India and now having been collected for a museum for public view. The lengthwise warp threads were hung from this, weighted at their lower ends and the weft threads interfaced to form a very rough cloth. A framework later replaced this crude loom which is now called a vertical loom and later switched over to the modern horizontal loom. Some scholars feel that the Egyptians invented the shuttle for holding the weft and to have attached the warp threads to two sticks in order to part the threads so that the shuttle could pass through. Good quality textiles imported from India and Far East were replacing the textiles in European and other countries. This gave an impetus to the mechanization of the loom and later inventions of the machine driven looms. The earlier process being hand operated was slow and could not cope with the increased demand for textiles and was replaced by machine in early 19$^{th}$ cent. AD and later by a high speed industrial loom.

According to a report cited in the Bibliography in 1773 John Kay introduced his "flying shuttle" which speeded up the weaving process. The first change in the spinning machines came in 1737 by Paul and Wyatt who invented the roller method of spinning eliminating the use of fingers. Later in 1764 and 1766 there were improvements to accommodate 100 spindles to make the production faster. After this there was no looking back for the Industrial revolution that followed which brought massive social and economic changes. By 19th cent. Britain was the greatest textile manufacturing country in the world. and it influenced India to a large extent when Indians were lured to use textiles from UK. However, in India .the traditional methods continued with modifications here and there due to it's impact but now after independence the government has helped the cottage industry to keep the traditional crafts alive with the result we still find many techniques of making textiles alive in India such as the applique decorated textiles, block printing, tie-dye is called *bandhana* in India (Plate 8) and *ikat* work of south India which is called *ikating* in Indonesia and *ikats* in Persia by the Turkic word *alejak,* batik the Javanese way of printing is also very much in vogue in south India, studded glass patch work of western India, tie and dye of Rajasthan, *Patolu* of Gujarat (Plate 9) and many others from this colorful country named India the land of diverse cultures. *Patolu* is woven with silken warp and weft, separately dyed by the tie and dyeing process. The warp is dyed separately and the weft separately marked at intervals with different dyes and tied with a cotton thread to prevent the dye for penetrating. Care is taken that in the loom, each of their colours of the warp and weft come exactly with the colour threads. This is a very laborious process and is a job of great skill. Jaipur is famous for tie and dye work and Cambay, Patan and Surat are famous for the manufacture of Patola.

CHAPTER III

# DETERIORATION OF TEXTILES

Textiles also degrade very easily and by nature they are perishable resulting into their total loss. It is very difficult to maintain the textiles once they start decaying or become weak due to normal wear and tear. In fact their decay starts the moment they are manufactured due to lack of their proper care and understanding. From the forgoing paragraphs it would now be easy to understand the mechanism of their decay and study the various parameters of decaying process. their organic nature and their inter action with the factors such as light, micro-organisms, acid and alkali composition. oxidation, air pollution, high temperature, changes in R.H., ageing, soiling, staining and insect attack making them weak, fragile, brittle, and powdery. Ultimately they break and fall apart especially if one of the warp or weft if they are not compatible with one another leaving either of them hanging loose.

There exposure to normal atmospheric conditions will cause textiles to weaken and disintegrate. The speed of the deterioration varies according to the environment and the nature of the fibers. The main factors that promote the decay of textiles are identified because textiles are organic, they are subject to attack by molds, micro-organisms bacteria and insects. Decomposition is greatest in situations that favor the growth of these organisms, such as damp heat, stagnant air, and contact of the material with vegetable matter. Attack by destructive insects may also be encountered. The ground reality is that what the environment could not do in centuries, the insects can do the harm in a very short time if once it starts. During the long span of my professional experience I have the knowledge of such a loss which could be avoided by the collection in-charges had they been vigilant enough. Excessive heat causes desiccation and embitterment; exposure to ultra-violet light causes a type of deterioration known as 'tendering,' as well as the photochemical degradation of susceptible dyes. Exposure to gases pollution can also cause tendering. In some cases, these gases are converted into acids, which are some of the main cause for the deterioration of textiles. We would now discuss their decay in detail.

## I. DECAY DUE TO ENVIRONMENT:-

The various environment which contribute to the decay of textiles include temperature, humidity, light, gaseous pollution, inherent factors, pests, unscientific storage and display, improper handling, transportation all contribute in the decay of textiles either alone or in conjunction with others.

### (1) LIGHT:-

Not only the visible light (violet and blue) but also the near UV radiations in day light which are invisible, high energy portion of the spectrum, that are emitted by the fluorescent tubes and are extremely harmful as they not only cause organic dyes to fade but also cause deterioration of the fiber structure resulting into oxidation from o level to higher levels. Exposure to both natural and artificial light can threaten the longevity of textiles. Visible light is the wave-length of light that is detected by the human eye. Textiles are highly susceptible to fading and structural degradation due to light exposure, Ultraviolet light is the invisible high-energy portion of the spectrum. Factors i.e. light intensity, the length of exposure to light and presence of UV radiations can cause cumulative damage to textiles which may become irreversible. It is capable of causing the greatest amount of damage within the shortest period of time. It has been reported that long exposure to UV radiations can even cause some textile fibers to turn yellow. Silk is damaged by light radiations at pH>10 and pH<4.

Rise in temperature accelerates the Photo Chemical decay. According to a study higher the temperature the more quickly fibers would age, as the chemical and photochemical reactions that cause aging accelerate as the temperature rises. Cotton degrades above 120 degree Celsius, wool degrades above 100 degree Celsius and silk degrades above 170 degree Celsius. Wool is little light sensitive and silk is up to four times more light sensitive than cotton. For reduction in tearing strength by 50% silk takes 200 hrs, cotton takes 940 hrs and wool takes 1200hrs.Many dyes used for dyeing textiles fade in light wavelengths between 300-500nm due to photochemical action of light. It is this region of light covering the near UV (300-400nm) and the violet and blue (400-500nm) which is most reactive to dyed textiles. It not only decays the dyes but also the material of the textile fibers. This action is two fold; the colour fades and the material support or fabric also disintegrates. It enhances in high humid and high temperature conditions. Thus the chemical change in the textile object caused by light also increases.

**(2) POLLUTION:-**

Pollution includes dust, dirt, stains and pollutant gases like oxide of sulphur, ozone, smoke and aerosol which originate from out door sources can get deposited in the fibres causing damage which may become very difficult to take care. On the other hand internal sources of damage could originate from wood, plastic, rubber, wood based paper, cardboard and newly painted surfaces which may emit acidic or alkaline fumes which not only degrade the textiles but also discolour them. Many old textiles are acquired by the museums in a dirty condition and have a smell of soiled textiles which promote biological activities. The textiles entering a collection come from diverse geographical backgrounds and habitats. Textiles have been used by their owners in the past and, therefore, may contain stains /spots of blood, body decomposition products, stains of food, grease, perspiration, and other varied composition. As a result grime obscures colours and textures, increasing the brittleness of the fibers with the result it becomes difficult to handle them safely without further damage. If dust contains gritty particles they will penetrate into the fabric and cut the fibers. Textiles tend to absorb sulphur di oxide from atmosphere which is converted into sulphurous acid which is unstable and ultimately gets converted into sulphuric acid responsible for wear and tear especially cotton is most affected. Wool and other Keratinaceous materials release sulphide gases at rates that increase with rise of temperature, humidity and light intensity.

## (3) TEMPRATURE AND RELATIVE HUMIDITY:-

Most of the textiles are affected by excessive dryness resulting from high temperature and low relative humidity thus weakening the structure of the fibers and making them brittle. High relative humidity is also equally deleterious causing weakness to the fabrics, growth of moulds resulting into permanent staining and weakening of sizing materials resulting in its loss. As a matter of fact the temperature and relative humidity of a closed space are interrelated. Climate inside a show case on the wall or in the gallery RH of a closed space increases if temperature drops and vice versa. Both extremes and fluctuations in them can cause damage to textile fibers. Most often the damages occur due to the expansion and contraction of the fibers in response to the drastic changes experienced by them. As long as the fibers are strong they can adjust themselves to the stress and strain thus being experienced by them but the situation changes on aging.

Textiles are hygroscopic and changes in humidity on a higher side produce the dimensional changes, they loose elasticity resulting into irreversible expansion of textiles if kept stretched or weighted at one end. On the other hand when humidity is on a lower side moisture content decreases and desiccation as well as brittleness happens resulting into loss of the mechanical strength, loss of flexibility and they also loose their natural feel.

**(4) BIOLOGICAL DECAY:-**

The biological agents that cause damage to textiles are mainly fungi and insects. They may stain, discolour, loss of coherence, attack on the lumen of natural fabrics and weaken them. It has been a general understanding that textiles of animal origin (Plate 10) are susceptible to insect damage more than the ones made from the plant materials. Cotton and linen are more susceptible to micro-organisms than the insects. Pests which are occasionally found on cellulose fibers include silver fish, crickets, cockroaches, and of course the termites. Barring termites which can destroy a wide range of fabrics containing cellulose, if they become the targets of their attack, the others are attracted to textiles because of the presence of sizing materials such as starch, dextrin, dyes and water repellants. Silver fish, Lepisma aaccharina is found to attack heavily starched cotton, linen, muslin and even sized silk. The house cricket, Acheta domesticus may eat plant fibers, silk etc. It is known to cause cuts of various length in fabrics. Cockroaches attack soiled and old textiles. Alkaline substrates are attacked by bacteria mould under humid conditions and on the other hand acidic substrates are attacked by fungi.

Fabrics made of animal hair especially wool attracts many species of insects which feed on them and digest Keratin with which hair is made of, they lay eggs in dark corners or ceases where they can remain un noticed & become active whenever climatic conditions are favorable for their growth. Studies made by Dr. S. M. Nair while he was in the M.S. University, Baroda and also Dr. Shashi Dhawan and others at the National Research Laboratory for Cultural Property, Lucknow, in India have identified species of cloth moth (Lepidoptera) it survives on proteinaceous material such as woolens and dermestid beetles that attack woolens. The most common pest in India is the case-bearing cloth moth, Tinea pellionella which destroys mainly woolen fabrics. The moth is brown in colour with three dark spots on the wings. The adults do not feed on textiles but it is its larvae that attack the woolen fabrics as they feel very hungry while they are becoming a pupa. It is strange that when they become adult they die. Carpet Beetles belong to the family Dermestidae of the insect order Coleoptera Antrenus vorex which feeds on hair, wool. Dermestid Beetles are known for their devastating attack on wool. Among those attacking woolen fabrics two species are most conspicuous as museum pests in India. These are Furniture-Carpet Beetle (Anthrenus flavipes)wooly bear and the Carpet Beetle (Attagenus gloriosae) and are very active in India. Termites (Isoptera) prefer textiles having cellulosic material. Cockroach (Blatta orientalis) damages wool.

Compared to wool, silk is a more stable material from the point of view of biodeterioration. The reason being that the insects do not like to eat its protein since they do not find any nutritive value in it. Though some insects may get attracted to silk also but for the sizing material and affinity for stains of a wide variety in them. Major pests feed on them but some of them thrive on the secondary substances present in them or because of the neighborhood materials stored near them and do accidental damage without really feeding on them.

## II. DECAY DUE TO INHERENT FACTORS:-

Very often when fibers of dissimilar composition are used for the warp and the weft it has been observed that one fiber survives at the cost of the other. For example if silk and wool have been used in the same textile and the silk has not been properly degumed before its use the acid content of the wool eats away the silk making it very much deteriorated whereas the wool fiber gets preserved. Many times Zari which is hard and heavy has been used in the same textile with silk fiber, it gets damaged due to friction while the textile if it is heavily brocaded (Plate 11) while it is worn or during its storage especially when it is kept folded for a long time in the same position. Here in this case a heavier material zari metallic fiber is in the company of a light weight material silk. Textiles by nature are usually stained easily while in use and unless cleaned immediately the fabric becomes not only dirty but it gets damaged at those spots. The textiles easily get soiled and attract biological factors of decay. Often fabrics are stitched for making dresses and their stitches get broken or become loose, thus separating the (Plate 12) individual parts of the dress, away from each other.

Tarnishing of the embroidery, the golden zari, due to the presence of copper and /or silver in the gold or presence of copper in silver zari often experiences their blackening which is due to an inherent process of its manufacturing. However, where ever tarnishing is not noticed it is evident that it is pure gold or silver. This is true in case of zari which was being manufactured earlier but the advent of it's artificial version of zari has changed the concept. Some dyes used for the block printing of textiles or moking them from the western India have inherent property of damaging the cotton or silk fabrics because of their acidic composition. (Plate 13) The prints look beautiful in the beginning but after some time the dye starts blackening followed by charring of the fabric which is seen at the back (Plate 14) of it. Later after the lapse of some more time the dye wherever it has been used for printing starts eating the cloth substrate. In the next stage we would be able to see the cracking and breaking of these printed parts resulting into perforations or loss.

## III. HANDLING DURING TRANSPORTATION AND STUDY:-

A considerable damage can happen to textiles when these are handled for examination or are in the stores for the study purposes by scholars time and again if adequate precautions are not followed of laying them on a flat surface of a table. Textiles should not be touched with wet and unclean hands. Clean gloves should be worn while these are being touched for one work or other and one should ensure that his/her hands are dry. Ink pens and markers are not to be used while making notes on them by the visiting scholars as ink stains are difficult to undo. To avoid such an accidental damage only pencils should be allowed in these areas. Textiles should not be piled one over the other and when transporting them to the laboratory or the photo studio or to the packing areas the textiles are well supported from beneath ensuring their safety. Every precaution should be taken that the textiles are not damaged due to careless handling (Plate 15) and wrong restoration by half backed conservators.

## IV. STAINING OF TEXTILES:-

Textiles may get stained due to several reasons such as (a) perspiration (b) blood (c) grease (d) excreta of insects(e) rust (f) smoke (g) soiling(h) particulate matter. These stains usually affect the aesthetic look. Some of these stains cause decay of materials depending on their nature besides disfiguring them. Stains are some times visually identifiable but can also be chemically identified. (1) Water stains which leave ring marks (2) Those resulting from liquid containing colouring matter (3) Those containing corrosive elements (a-c above) which attack the fibers as well as decay them and (4) Solid deposits (d-h above). Exact nature and chemistry must be found out of the stains, their effect on the material of the textile and by products produced by the stains.

## V. STORAGE AND DISPLAY:-

Most of the Curators may feel that nothing can happen to the textiles while in storage or on display. They at times casually mention in their lectures that such and such artifact is preserved in such and such collection. I must emphasize here once again that preservation does not happen simply because of its physical presence in a collection. Preservation as well as decay is continuing even after development of technical and scientific technology and has to be managed well according to the latest thinking on the subject. Selection of the storage area is to be done very judiciously, it has to have full lighting, ventilation/ air circulation to avoid any stagnant surroundings (Plate 16) and it should be away from the air conditioning plants and water or sewerage pipelines in those areas which are still in the low lying areas, the basement has to be avoided.

As a conservation personnel who, over five decades, has been an active as a practical conservator first in the Archaeological Survey of India and later selected for the National Museum, Conservation Department, New Delhi since early 1958 when it was in its infancy and now with the establishment of the National Museum Institute, A Deemed University by way of a Visiting Guest Faculty for teaching Art conservation (theory and practice) to young student conservators can make the above statement sure and meaningful. Perhaps it would not be out of context to mention that it has been a pretty long innings for me from 1954 to 1991 while I was holding various governmental positions and further to this date. I see many of my students have been doing very well in the profession. It makes me real happy to hear and see even from a distance that so and so who studied in the NMI is doing well. For me they are still the same and I do see myself in them even now towards the fag end of my life and the professional career since they would always carry forward the messages of preventive and curative conservation, which I have been actively teaching them.

## VI. ENVIRONMENTAL CONTROL:-

The proper storage and display can certainly provide protection from the factors that lead to decay which could be avoided if the techniques to prevent decay are followed in letter and spirit. Environmental control methods through AC are the best especially the central air conditioning with 24 hours operation, if it can be maintained, is the ideal. The RH and temperature throughout the year is recommended (Thomson 1978) to be 55% $\pm$ 4% and temperature 20$\pm$1.5 degree Celsius. with a provision of air filters of at least 60% efficiency and activated carbon filters to check $SO_2$ not to exceed 10mg/mm$^3$. Unless the environmental conditions can be controlled within each case, they should be designed for primary ventilation through filtered openings or holes, covered with cloth, cotton batting or other filtering material.

Out of the two i.e. the display showcases and the storage cases of Textiles are the backbone of the museum activity since the majority of artifacts usually remain stored in the storage cupboards all along the year, unless rotated frequently, for longer periods than in any exhibition galleries. The textile collection is also required to be examined periodically to check any possible source of damage before it is too late for which the curator has to repent later. The storage area also needs fire fighting equipment with alarm system is installed to check any such problem. There are some basic factors of textiles decay which have to be well understood. The first precaution to be taken is that the textiles in good condition have to be segregated from those which are not in good shape (Plate 17) and to remain confined at one place so that the infection does not spread .The next precaution is to separate the textiles material wise, size and shape wise. On this would depend the type of the storage or display that is appropriate for the different types of textiles to protect them from any physical/mechanical deterioration. Costumes would need different storage than carpets, sarees, rugs, wall hangings etc. The storage have to be inspected at regular intervals so that any damage could be noticed immediately and it could be avoided well in time before it is too late. The types of storage, I am talking include flat storage for each one of them in drawers, rolled on rollers and on padded hangers. Heavy weight costumes to be placed on dummies and mannequins to get full body support. This will not only retrieve them quickly but would be conservation oriented since there is a need to evaluate and reorganize our storage procedures as per latest thinking to save them from any unwanted damage while in the storage. Flat storage minimizes the fiber damage in which drawers, trays, shelves and boxes are suggested made of acid-free, lignin-free boxes including baked enamel metal shelving units.

Folding of textiles have to be stopped. In case folding becomes unavoidable folded areas should be padded with acid free tissue or polyester batting to take care of the folds. Large size carpets, rugs and other big size textiles can be rolled on rollers keeping the decorative side facing outside on the roller. Acid free tissue spacers should be used on the front side. Hangers made of good quality plastic with suitable padding can be used for costumes and dresses.

Similarly our methods of display and conservation handling also need critical evaluation to minimize any probable decay and modify the techniques as per latest technology so that any unintentional damage could also be checked before it happens.(Plate 18 & 19) The first and foremost is to check the intensity of illumination as per international standards. Many at times the Presentation officers may prefer very bright lights to highlight his/her work which is harmful for the fugitive dyes and some fibers also. Hence the need to control the lights. We should realize here that the display lights in a market place and in an exhibition of artifacts can not be copied in a museum because the aims of the two are different. In museum exhibitions the main aim is to have a compromise so as to deter the damage which though may be slow but is not desirable even if the illumination may look dim. In a market place they need to brightly illuminate their products to boost up their sale. We have to plan for their safety in the long run whereas their approach is up to the point the textile is sold.

To achieve the aim of reducing the harmful effect of light radiations we should aim for controlling the light .The first step is to know that sun light is most damaging for textiles. The next step is to use artificial light source so that one could take necessary action to minimize the intensity of the light source, followed by restricting the exposure period to minimum and take action to reduce/ eliminate the photo chemical action of light having UV and visible radiations as far as possible. For textiles it should be around 50 Lux. There is a need to monitor the extant of colour change associated with the display and take appropriate action accordingly. Under museum conditions the fading of dyes is to be checked especially in India. This could be monitored by using a Minolta 'Chroma Meter' CR-200 portable tristimulus colour analyzer. To keep the lighting conditions under check we could use Acrylic or polycarbonate sheet or thin acetate foil. We may also use plastic or glass filters by coating them with one of the chemicals such as zinc white or titanium dioxide or lead white. It is also advisable to use Venetian blinds or dark curtains in the display area. In the stores we may have the light switches outside them so that the lights are used only when some work is being done in them otherwise it is better to keep the textiles in dark. Lighting system based on fiber optics have to be introduced as soon as possible.

Some of the display methods are namely (i) framing (ii) hanging and (iii) use of mannequins. We may display small textiles still in good condition flat, framing or display in a table show case is best. However, fragile textiles should not be framed. Such textiles should be given a backing first to be attached to a rigid support and/or framing. Care should be taken to use spacers between the glass and the frame so that there is a breathing space. Double sided tape or Velcro support system should be used very judiciously to avoid nails. A large textile if it is to be displayed against a wall it should not touch the wall and also it should be properly framed with a starch free muslin cloth backing.

Despite limitations of the Oddy tests, done by the British Museum Research Laboratory, London, remain the only means of testing the suitability of storage and display materials in a simple and inexpensive way. It is a hard fact that all materials decay with time but because of some synthetic materials used in the fabrication of storage cases and showcases for display may do more harm than good because of a large amount of additives used in their manufacture can liberate fumes and emit harmful vapours which would aggravate the decay process. Tarnishing of zari, fading/change of colours, if they contain lead contents, it may change them to grayish white or black. Knowledge about safe materials to be used in display exhibitions and storage cases, therefore, would go a long way to eliminate the danger posed by rubber, bakelite and certain plastics such as cellulose nitrate contain sulphur or which produce NOX. Some paints e.g. the latex base paints and pigments which contain sulphur if used in display cases would tarnish the Zari of the textiles brocaded with metallic threads. Some timbers especially when new, emit gases those produce tannic acid or formic acid which would decay cotton and linen. Newly built buildings produce alkaline aerosols which decay silk.

So it is not only the textiles which decay slowly under normal atmospheric conditions but in the hasty decisions to make exhibitions more glamorous or to mount them quickly the presentation personnel may harm unintentionally the textiles. Decay which took a long time to affect the textiles due to the environmental parameters of decay and could not do the harm in centuries or in decades would do it in the bad company of synthetic materials, having harmful contaminants in no time. The problems of this nature are due to lack of technical information about commercial products, particularly about the sudden introduction of new materials in the manufacturing process could be overcome if enough interaction and sharing of information between the conservators and the manufacturers is debated in conferences and seminars or is made available to the conservators well before their actual use.

## VII. PHYSICAL/MECHANICAL DECAY:-

The animal fibers consist primarily of protein and are more resistant to decay than vegetable fibers, which are composed primarily of cellulose. Flax and cotton, for example, are very susceptible to attack by bacteria under humid conditions and seldom survive in archaeological environments. They withstand moderate alkaline conditions because of their cellulose content, but are readily affected by acids. Moisture easily passes through the fibers of linen, causing the material to undergo dimensional and weight changes as well as changes in the overall strength. Physical decay includes change in shape, density, surface morphology and moisture regain etc. and the mechanical deterioration includes the alterations of tensile strength, tensile strain, extensibility, elastic limit, modulus, flexibility and the usual feel of the textiles.

Many times the textiles are physically damaged due to folding resulting into creases, use of iron nails to tack them and making holes, wrong mounting, framing, undue stretching leading to undue wear and tear and continuous hanging in one position making physically weak a particular part due to weight in case of very heavy textiles. Support is needed when there is considerable weakness in the yarn of the textile which needs repair by way of insertion of a new material usually behind the original either in full or in patches using a needle and thread.

**VIII. CHEMICAL DECAY:-**

The chemical formula of Cellulose has been shown in this book $(C_6H_{10}O_5)_n$, and the general formula for Wool can be simplified as C-O-H-N-S and for Silk it could be expressed as C-O-H-N. Wool and silk, are built up from amino acid units into polypeptides which link together to form protein. Amino acids have the properties of both amines(base) and carboxylic acids. There are many amino acids which can be combined to form larger molecules with different compositions. The two simplest amino acids make up a large bulk of silk fiber (fibroin) with sericin. They are cross linked and are generally aligned parallel to the fiber axis. The high crystalline nature of the fiber is supposed to provide strength to silk. Wool is largely constituted of keratin, a polypeptide made of different amino acids. Due to a particular arrangement into long molecules which contribute to extensibility.

Cellulose is sensitive to attack by acids which, can result in hydrolysis. This produces hydrocellulose which is very weaker substance than cellulose. The progressive attack produces a break in the molecular chain at the 1,4, glycolic acidic link, liberating both reducing and non reducing groups and with a loss of resistance, transforming the fiber eventually into friable dust. Cellulose is weakened from attack with strong bases and reagents with a loss of weight and a progressive deterioration which is a function of the number of aldehyde groups present. Seriously degraded cellulose is partially water soluble. Besides this there are many acidic dyes which has been used in the cotton textiles such as black dye, which chars it first and later eats it away resulting into holes and perforations. (Plate 20) This aspect needs further study of the dyes

Protein fibers e.g. in wool the peptide link is chemically strong but can be broken by hydrolysis, by pepsin and other enzymes. Wool can absorb acid in small concentrations. However, strong acids attack peptide groups in the chain and degrade textiles and manifest in loss of tensile strength (wool is stretched) and depends on the acids and their concentration. On the other hand alkalis can start hydrolysis in wool more drastically and even 5% caustic soda destroys it completely. Silk when treated with acids and alkalis, starts hydrolysis of the peptide bonds between pH4 and pH8. The degradation in the fiber is seen in the form of loss of tensile strength. Acids produce more harm than alkalis. Oxidizing agents attack the protein as the damage is very vigorous and decays it mostly in the sides of the chain, in the terminal amino groups and in the peptide bonds also. Oxidation is caused by the activated oxygen of the air and produces oxycellulose. This process is hastened by factors such as (i) contact with oxidizing agents e.g. drying oils which form peroxides (ii) contact with metals such as iron acting as a catalytic agent-rust in textiles and (iii) photolysis by short wave radiations such as burning of curtains exposed to sunlight. Carbonyl sulphides the most important of the sulphides and the agent likely to be responsible for tarnishing of silver and copper in the storage. The tarnishing is caused by the action of sulphur compounds present in atmosphere on the silver substrate of gold embroideries. A fresh ,aqueous solution of sodium hydro sulphite (20-25 g./litre) with tri sodium phosphate (4-5 g/litre) is found effective in removing tarnish from gold threads. Tarnished pieces are immersed in solution at 65-70$^0$ C for 2-3 seconds or more if required. For embroideries with woolen backings 1g./liter of gelatin should be added to the solution. It has been noticed that this does not happen in the display galleries because of human bio-effluents are potentially more significant sources.

## CHAPTER IV

# EXAMINATION AND DOCUMENTATION

It is needless to mention that examination and recording of the findings is very necessary so that we can record it's condition and also consult it later in order to monitor the health of the object at short intervals and what is it's reaction to the treatment executed on the object. It would also help the future conservators in evaluating the results and the scheme of future conservation that may be necessary at that point of time. In the past when no proper records were made or were not available it often was very embarrassing situation and a waste of time if the chemical analysis to know what has been done on the object in the past and evaluate the changes in object and the materials used in conservation.

After examination, therefore, it was necessary to record the various aspects of it's present condition. Now the question behind the examination is what we want to record. These findings in a tabulated form for future reference are to be filled in the form as per Appendix I. The object has to be identified, what it is made from, what is it's method of making, what is it's condition, whether it has been restored in the past, how dirty it is and what are the deposits chemically, what are the alterations (physical, chemical, mechanical and biological). We must save what is contemporary to the object and keep a record of what is added later. It is preferred to have faithful and detailed photography before, during if necessary and after conservation. The results of a good quality Digital Camera are to be taken for records. It is always preferred to have Documentation in three ways textual, graphic and photographic using visible and at times invisible radiations also.

This would streamline the procedures of the conservation techniques which have been undertaken at this stage so that suitable methodology could be chalked out. for future reference. This would result in understanding the textile and it's problems better so that what exactly is needed for the object could be done. (a) the nature of the fibers (b) the spin of the yarn (i.e., 'Z' or 'S' twist) (c) the number of wefts and warps per inch (or centimeter) (d) the type of weaving and of dye (water-fast or soluble) (e) paint dye or mineral (f) metal threads, and any other features that may be diagnostic or of interest for research by all the Musicologists, Conservators and Art Historians.

CHAPTER V

# STEPS IN CONSERVATION

The conservation and restoration of textiles is a specialized field. For successful work a thorough knowledge of the raw materials and of the different production techniques is essential. Conservation practices seek to understand and preserve the tangible cultural property in its content, where as conservation ethics seek to understand and preserve the intangible cultural value hidden in them. Having observed textiles of Indian origin in many collections abroad, we in India are concerned with their preservation for posterity as a whole, irrespective of their present location since they represent the spirit of India and art is not confined to a nation since it is truly international of the human race. To me, therefore, an ethical approach is required by the conservators irrespective of their geographical locations to choose materials and techniques which are being added to these textiles and see that the techniques being adopted are compatible with them so that we do not loose their original feel and spirit of Indian origin.

At this stage the complete scheme based on the scientific examination leading to conservation should be available and this scheme should stand on the reasoning. At this point of time the Conservator would know, not only what is to be done but also what is not to be done. The actual conservation depends on a particular textile and is specific to this one under treatment.

(a) Eradication of the past infection due to insects and micro-organisms by a proper insecticide and fungicidal treatment.
(b) Chemical cleaning after dry cleaning /vacuum cleaning.
(c) Consolidation for restoring it's present strength.
(d) Physical repairs.
(f) Restoration.
(g) Preventive Measures.

## 1. ERADICATION OF PAST BIODETERIORATION:-

The textiles have been acquired for a the collection from various geographical locations and it is just possible that in the past these suffered an attack of the insects and micro-organisms. The activity may be dormant at present but the eggs of the insects can hatch during favorable climatic conditions any time. However, if the infection is active and visible the first thing to do is to segregate them from others which are still in good condition. Some institutions are fumigating all objects coming to their collection at the time of entry and repeating fumigation at regular intervals. For the protection against fungi and bacteria are possible (1) inhibiting the activity of enzymes; (2) physical protection of fibers; (3) chemical modification of fibers, and use of toxic chemicals. For ancient textiles only the last method has a practical application. For wholesale treatment of mold and insect infestation, we have to place the infested objects in a closed container with thymol crystals. The crystal can be vaporized by the use of a radiation electric heating bulb under the watch glass container having thymol $C_{10}H_{14}O$ chemically known as Isopropyl cresol crystals. After treatment with thymol crystals, we can also spray the objects with a chemical which is reported safe 0.5-1 percent Lysol solution. This treatment will remedy most problems. A mixture 1:1Carbon disulfide $CS_2$ and carbon tetrachloride $CCl_4$ can also be used as a fumigation agent if the infection has been active in the recent past. Sulfural fluoride $SO_2 F_2$ gas fumigation was being done at the Smithsonian Support Center, Maryland, U.S.A. for fumigation of organic artifacts with the entire satisfaction of all concerned.

It has been reported that Disinfectant solution can be prepared in the lab by mixing 0.1 percent Dowicide 1 (ortho-phenyl phenol), 68 percent ethanol, and 30 percent de-ionized water. This solution is lethal to most bacteria, fungal spores, and surface mildews. Dowicide 1 a commercial product has a maximum solubility of 0.1 percent in water and 46-58 percent in the various alcohols. Alternatively, a solution of 2 percent Dowicide A and sodium ortho-phenylphenate can be used. Dowicide A has a maximum solubility of 120 percent in water and approximately 350 percent in alcohol. For the majority of textile disinfectant needs, Lysol disinfectant spray will suffice. Lysol spray consists of 0.1 percent Dowicide1, 79 percent ethanol, 8 percent n-alkyl, and 0.035 percent n-ethyl morpholinium ethylsulfates (deodorizers and scents). The conservator should keep in mind that topical treatments are not long lasting. It has been reported that fumigation by Anoxia fades textiles dyed with Prussian blue because it reduces it, but the fading might spontaneously reverse on re-exposure to air but does not reverse in some other variety of Prussian blue. It was, therefore, recommended that Ageless anoxic fumigation should not be used for textiles dyed with Prussian blue, since deteriorated dye may or may not recover from fading. Fumigation by chemicals these days is not only hazardous since it does pollute the environment in general but it is also harmful for the Conservators in the lab who have to work on them. The Conservators today are more conscious about the hazards connected with it. Allover the globe, therefore, attempts are being made to find alternates which would be environment friendly.

One of the attempts have been the use of Ageless Oxygen scavenger. Which is reported lethal to a wide range of insects at their various development stages since it reduces the oxygen concentration to less than0.05% in the atmosphere inside the chamber. Oxygen Scavenger is prepared from powdered Iron Oxide which rapidly absorbs atmospheric oxygen. It is reported as an alternative to nitrogen gas packing and is described as a safe means of inhibiting the aerobic micro-organism growth and as a means of killing insect activity. Second method which I tried while in office was the technique of Radiological control which is also called as Sterile Insect Technique in which we use dangerous Gamma rays radiations from a cobalt 60 source(5-10KR) irradiation which would reduce the fertility. Eggs that hatch would produce larve with extensive chromosomal aberrations resulting into delayed inherited semi- sterility. This in return would decrease the multiplication rate of insects by making males incapable of producing and the eggs laid by females would not hatch. Yet another way of control is the use of Natural biocides which are known to Indians from a long time. One such product Neem (Melia azadirachta) has a good potential in India where its seed, leaf and other products are being used. It is also called as "Sarva roga nivarini". Neem leaves contain Carboxy methyl Steroid ($C_{30}H_{36}O_9$ and many biocides from which have been patented abroad by synthesizing its chemical constituent Quercetin $C_{15}H_{10}O_7$ which is anti insects, anti fungus and anti bacteria. Azadirachta indica, Neemix, Bioneem and margosane are produced from it. A plant for production of insecticide with US collaboration has been established at Tumkur near Bangalore from neem seeds. De-oiled seeds of neem are crushed and is reacted repeatedly with hexane to remove oil which has been found very effective against Dermestidae: coleoptera (Anthrenus vorax). Some insecticides like Nimbin has been found very effective against Powder post beetle attacking wood and bamboo and Grastrillus indicus damaging the Palm leaf manuscripts. Dried neem leaves have been used in remote Indian locations for keeping insects away from textiles such as Carpets.

Side by side with it, many natural products are being used all over India for keeping many insects away especially from manuscripts such as tobacco, Vitex negundo, camphor, black cumin seeds, roots of sweet flag, Turmeric roots of a shrub(Curcuma longa), snake slough and feathers of peacock, Orpiment, Realgar, Cloves, Pepper, Indian lemon grass oil (Cymbopogon sp.), Citronela grass oil (Cymbopogon nardus), du du oil (ballon vine heart seed), Dummela oil (Fossil resin) are being used as insect repellent. These should be studied chemically and then used. It goes without saying that this branch of science needs further evaluation and research to study these indigenously available materials.

## 2. CHEMICAL CLEANING:-

After the fumigation is complete, unless it has been done under vacuum, there is a great need to take adequate safety precautions so that the infection does not spread to other places in the premises. The dry brushing of textiles is the first step and it is a very delicate operation and care should be taken so that there are no physical damages to the fragile textile items. The residues from the fumigation have to be disposed off very carefully. The dust is light weight, dry and loose particles. Care should be taken to use a screen/gauze to protect the fabric from suction. There are a number of ways one can use to modify the vacuum cleaner to make it suitable for conservation works. The micro vacuum attachment Kit is very useful for vacuuming of fragile textiles with some precautions. Usually textiles are received in a lot for fumigation, however, further conservation would vary from textile to textile and, therefore, the final examination /documentation is done followed by analysis of the stains and by finding out of their solubility/ swelling. Treatment which is better in its swelling rather than dissolving. Individual needs would depend on the nature of the stains. Other considerations of low toxicity, penetration and retention are some other of the solutions on the surface, safety of the workers. Instead of solubility by one solvent we may try a workable mixture. Even enzymes, sequestering and detergents are some other better solutions. Loose surface dust collects over the exposed surface, folds, seams and at the back. A great number of foreign accumulation substances can be removed from the textiles by simply washing the textile in water. De-ionized water is always preferred. If washing and dry cleaning are both necessary the dry cleaning should come first, as its possible drying effect will be counteracted by washing. Ingrained dust can only be removed by the use of a fluid. Greasy dirt can only be removed by a detergent mixed with water or a solvent, stains due to discoloration which usually formed by breaking of the polymer chains in the textile fibers whether cellulosic or proteinus. Author has a long experience of handling the cleaning of a large number of textiles in this order. If necessary, we may add 1% neutral non-ionic detergent such as Lissapol N to remove dirt and soil. Micaela Sousa and Maria Joao Melo along with some others, in 2005 have described a new method of cleaning instead of watery using supercritical carbon dioxide (SC $CO_2$) as a dry cleaning solvent of old silk textiles and the method was found very safe for cleaning very deteriorated silk textiles. They mention its use on a 18th cent. textile sample and report that cent per cent safety was ensured to the fragile textile. The physical integrity of the fiber was preserved and the metal ions were not disturbed. Every one in conservation field would be eagerly awaiting their further study and treatment for cleaning the dirt and other undesirable accumulations from the historic clothes of Virgin and child. Cleaning the stains is an irreversible process. The cleaning of historical textile always involves some form of compromise between effective soil removal and the damage that can be caused by a cleaning process during the washing and cleaning process. We should always identify the nature of the stains. We have first to decide whether to remove the stain by spot clean, solvent clean, wet clean or do nothing. The obstinate stains sensitivity of fibers, finishes with various solvents and reagents to be checked first and there after it can be bleached in a weak solution of hydrogen peroxide solution. Removal of individual spot stains is difficult to achieve without either leaving a cleaner patch in the surroundings or creating a ring mark. Spotting or suction tables are used to give an effective results. For more stubborn stains (including mildew, mold, black sulfide stains, and organic stains), we can soak the artifact in mixture of 60ml 30% hydrogen peroxide and 2.5% sodium silicate solution in 100 ml hot de-ionized water all together in 1000cc of de-ionized water.

Textile conservation vacuum suction table may be used for local stain removal. Some conservators prefer washing first as it depends on the overall scheme that has been decided in advance for the treatment. Various other formulations are reported in the literature for stain removal but these are to be used very judiciously. Sodium silicate and meta silicate are stabilizers, which are added to control the decomposition of hydrogen peroxide ($H_20_2$) to water ($H_20$). Whenever possible, a simple solution of hydrogen peroxide (and possibly a stabilizer) is recommended for stain removal because as the hydrogen peroxide loses oxygen, it bleaches and converts to water. Therefore, there is no danger of continuing chemical action. Hydrogen peroxide can be used on all vegetable fibers and its bleaching effect is permanent. We avoid use of hydrogen peroxide on hair or any fiber that was not white when originally in use. Textiles with iron rust stains can be treated with any of the chemical solution (1) 5% oxalic acid $(COOH)_2$, (2) 5 percent EDTA disodium, (3) 5 percent acetic acid $CH_3COOH$, (4) 5 percent formic acid (HCOOH) and (5) 2-10 percent ammonium citrate. Oxalic acid and hydrofluoric acid solutions are the most effective for removing iron stains from archaeological textiles. Extreme caution must be taken, however, when handling hydrofluoric acid. EDTA disodium and ammonium citrate solutions are often recommended because their higher pH (>2.5) potentially do less damage to fibers. These solutions are effective but are rather slow. After any chemical treatment, intensive rinsing in de-ionized water will remove all the residue from the textile which may adversely affect the fibers over a period of time. INTACH, Lucknow (1996) has reported the use of a solution mixture of (i)

Sodium Hydroxide–5gms. (2) Sodium Carbonate (anhydrous) — 5gms. (3) Hydrogen per oxide--50ml. And (4) Sodium meta sulphate (anhydrous) —50gms. In this method the quantity of solution is taken on the basis of the dry weight of the cloth from which the stains have to be removed. The dry weight of the Kurta was 85gms. and the solution taken was 850 ml. For the cleaning of a Lucknow, cotton Kurta with chikan embroidery work having stains similar to foxing marks was treated by soaking it in this mixture for 10 minutes only and the result was successful. Similar solutions have been used abroad with success by Donny L. Hamilton, Conservation Research Laboratory, Texas A&M University USA. It is thus advised that these formulations may have succeeded in these individual cases and need to be used only after experimentation based on full understanding of the science behind it. The attempt should not lead to over cleaning. It is better to dim down the stains rather their total removal. Sodium per borate (2 oz per gallon; 10g per lire) with a little detergent in an enamel bath were used to soak a silken dress which was heated near boiling point at which oxygen was liberated. The heat was then turned off and the water left to cool.

For textiles that cannot be cleaned with water (such as textiles with water soluble dyes), dry cleaning using organic solvents, such as per chlorethylene or tri chlorethylene, or petroleum solvents, such as white spirits, is recommended. The advantages of solvent cleaning are many. (1) Unlike water, solvents do not soften textile fibers, minimizing the risk of shrinkage and loss of shape. (2) Dyes not fast in water may be undisturbed in solvent. (3) Solvents are more efficient than water for dissolving grease. (4) In general, solvents are volatile and dry quickly. To combine the advantages of washing with dry cleaning detergents (emulsifiers) and a very small amount of water are generally added by the Drycleaner along with benzene and gasoline etc. used for doing the job. Cleaning of embroidered textiles needs a detailed study of the technique of it's making to understand the intricacies of the work firs including the analysis of the various components. Usually dry brushing with special brushes of hard materials for cleaning is done first. This method would certainly clean the metal of tarnishing. The question arises whether the embroidered textiles could be cleaned with water. The metal thread invariably has a textile core. If this is being cleaned to take care of the tarnishing the textile as a whole should not be treated with water as it might damage the thread inside. According to the latest study conducted by Margareta Bergstrand and Erika Hedhammar 2006 none of the attempts to clean such textiles with plasma, laser, chemical, mechanical or electro chemical are fully satisfactory for the metal and the textile fiber combined. In my opinion, therefore, it needs further study by which we can save the metal and also not damage the thread inside.

### 3. STRENGTHENING OF TEXTILES:-

After the cleaning, the next stage is to repair, support and consolidation in order to ensure it's safety in the Storage and Display. (Vargas 2005) has shown in the form of a Poster, the reinforcing treatment of silk threads with carboxy methyl chitosan and chitosan acetate which form transparent, flexible, air and water permeable films with moisturizing, adhesive and antibacterial and anti fungal properties. The study seems to be interesting and the conservators at large would await the detailed study before it could be used on a large scale. In addition their polarity and amino character make them chemically compatible with proteins such as silk. The attempt is to do only what is really necessary as in the case of cleaning. There are some textiles which for one reason or the other, can not be sewn, (Plate 21) although, for those textiles which are physically strong, sewing is the least destructive and most easily reversible strengthening technique The main procedures for the strengthening of weak textiles in India is by providing a new support after proper cleaning which is tacked to the original textile by stitching and darning using the needle and thread to pass between the threads and through them eliminating any further scope of inflicting damage to the textile. (Plate 22 & 23) By this method the threads of the old textile are relieved of the strain and at the same time detached fragments, loose threads, holes, frayed edges and the like are secured to the backing. The supporting cloth should match with the original in structure ,and if possible also in material. Stitching the support at the back of the old textile is preferred in India because it does not affect the flexibility and the feel of a textile. (Plates 24 & 25, 26 & 27, 28 & 29) The textiles when reinforced in this way it is partly sharing the stress and strain of the old textile while handling them during storage, transportation and exhibitions. It is reversible as the stitches can be easily undone any time. The only disadvantage is that it is a very laborious, time consuming technique besides being costly. Moreover, in India the traditional Textile Craftsmen work on their knees while doing embroidery or undertake repair by darning. The National Museum, New Delhi still traditionally prefers this time tested method. However, to overcome this I had introduced a Loom type stand for this type of problem. I am happy to say that this new technique has solved the problem easily. The main reason behind it was that in the past all textiles have been produced on a hand driven loom and new system of repair of textiles works on the same principle. The large size textiles after the initial tacking of the textile to be tacked to the new support, it could go on the loom like stand, can be rolled and only that part is unrolled while it is being restored at a particular point of time. The so called loss during repair which include re-stitching of the split seams, the restoration of the dislodged decorations, taking care of the local weakness and damage such as tears and restoration of the fastenings etc., has thus been mostly eliminated. Smaller textiles are also being stretched on to a simple frame and worked without rolling them after the day's work. This is the safest method for the valuable textiles according to our experience in India.

Often, the only solution of reinforcing fragile textiles is to support them with a synthetic mesh of terylene, light cotton fabric like muslin or other compatible material. Starches have been used since I joined the National Museum Laboratory in 1958 and earlier in the Central Asian Antiquities Museum (ASI) (Plate 30, 31 & 32) under the able guidance of Late T.R. Gairola. Particularly fragile textiles are sometimes mounted in between sheets of plexi glass or of a plain glass. Over the years a large number of adhesives which are available for this work commercially have been used .

Those which have been used for mounting of textiles fall in three groups (1) contact; (2) water soluble; (3) thermoplastic. The first type of adhesive ie. the contact type is not suitable since it is rubber based and is reported to become insoluble with time. It also deteriorates and may also pass on the damage to the valuable textile that is required to be strengthened. Those in the second type need the application of pressure during drying. It is necessary to ensure that the colours are not affected by water and that the weave structure of the textile is not disturbed by the adhesive traveling up to the front. At this point of time adhesives of the third type seem to be the best out of the lot.

In most cases, a heat-seal adhesive, such as polyvinyl acetate, polyvinyl alcohol, Acryloid B-72, or their emulsions, are used to coat the backing which is then ironed (heat-sealed) to the textile. Any breaks in the threads either in the warp or weft of the material should be affixed with drops of adhesive to prevent additional unraveling. The Conservator also has the option to consolidate and reinforce fragile textiles with various synthetic resins. Water softens and makes textile fibers pliable, emulsions and water-soluble resins are preferred for textile consolidation. Lithuanian Art Museum Scientists in their recent study of Acrylic adhesive used for strengthening of fragile silk textiles have concluded on the basis of SEM investigations and studied the properties of silk fibers such as fibrillation, partial or full breaking of silk filament, and the effect of the adhesive support technique. The further studies of Ms. Ragauskiene were continuing to come to further conclusive results at the Vilnius University and we would await her findings. Another very interesting case study of re-valuation and re-treatment of an English court mantua of the 1740s, in the collection of V&A, London which was to be displayed in it's new British Galleries has been discussed in details and reported in the Studies in Conservation in it's Vol.51, No.2 (2006). Water-based adhesives also give the conservator more 'working time' than solvent-based adhesives. The most frequently recommended resins for textile conservation which are being used abroad are: 1. polyvinyl alcohol (water-soluble, dries clear with minimum shrinkage) 2. polyvinyl acetate (V7) (note: resin shrinkage during drying may distort fibers) 3. ethulose (ethyl-hydroethyl cellulose) (water-soluble, very pliable) 4. polymethacrylate 5. Acryloid B-72, 5 percent in toluene. A mixture of 0.15 percent ethyl-hydroethyl cellulose, 0.6 percent polyethylene glycol (PEG) 400, and 0.2 percent fungicide will consolidate fragile fabrics and restore moisture to dry,brittle fibers. A solution of 20 percent lanolin in toluene can be applied to fibers that have a tendency to shred or lint. These are some methods used abroad. The only disadvantage is that it is not fully reversible since the adhesive goes deep into the fibers and often may cause discoloration and embrittlement. An adhesive which has the minimal shrinkage or is shrinkage free and it should not harden on drying is the best. One of the most needed requirement is that the textile after mounting should remain soft, pliable and should not alter its physical feel. It is a matter for further research whether the new supporting cloth should be similar in composition as of the old support.

However, the new trend these days is to use some synthetic materials such as nylon net or terylene etc. There is no one opinion on this issue. The point to consider that the colour, strengthened texture of the new support should be very near to the original one and if necessary the new support can be aged artificially keeping in view the dissimilarity of the two in mind as regards their expansion and contraction is concerned. They should be compatible with each other.

This artificial ageing of the new support is being experimented in Japan by using Electron Beam Radiation for this purpose. We in the National Museum, New Delhi have been providing silk support to silk, muslin or markeen or dusuti to cotton and rafal to woolen textiles. We also see that the new support is thin, flexible, strong and light in weight than the original it has to support. It is nevertheless left for the future researchers to find out if the artificial ageing of the supporting cloth remains useful in the long run or not one of the latest techniques is of NAP bonding. adhesive is applied on the material using a screen of mesh so that only the minimal amount of adhesive is used for lining/ mounting. The preliminary experiments using Ethulose has shown good results as it does not change the softness and remains pliable as reported in the para just above.

However, in respect of some fragile fragments from Central Asia and south America we have used other method of strengthening called pasting and dry mounting. Long time back I did some further work to mount the fragmentary textile pieces from the Central Asian collection of the National Museum, New Delhi by a process which I called as dry mounting in which chiffon gauge of the size of the fragment was first stretched on a wooden frame and later coated with Callilac (PVA Solution) diluted in a suitable solvent so as to get the required viscosity. It was allowed to dry and then the textile fragment was tacked on the new support using a slightly hot electric iron at 60-70 degree Celsius to it. It was later removed from the frame and mounted in between two mounts (acid free) as is done in case of miniature paintings. The advantage of this process is that we can see it's back and study it. Most of the conservators abroad favored spraying of equal amount of AYAA and AYSC making a 10% solution in toluene which was later on the basis of experience was switched over to a 30% stock solution made in toluene with ethanol preferably using a vacuum table.

It has been pointed out by various Conservators to have one or the other disadvantages. They objected making further needle holes in the original while stitching new support onto the old. Many people feel that most of the treatments make the aged textile more stiff and the weight also increases. IIC abstracts 5334 suggests using minute droplets of glue, put between threads in a few central points, and thin threads glued on the left side(across tears and hanging threads, and around frayed edges) have been found sufficient to consolidate the weave in a very inconspicuous way. The greatest advantage of this is that it is reversible easily. It was desirable to achieve maximum flexibility and restore adequate strength to the weakened textile.

Dr. D. Lehmann from the Berlin State Museum, Berlin (Studies in conservation, 1964) suggested "that no supporting fabric is required for strengthening the old flags as these are simply sprayed on both sides with a plastic in solution. Heavy flags and those with defects are supported by backing them with a material such as Perlon monofilament fabric, using a solution of 'propenoate' as glue. The particular advantage of this method is that material is much more resistant to aging than natural silk and also more resistant to tearing. A sewn support causes damages to the fragile textile due to stitch holes and to the chafling effect." He has, however, not disclosed the chemical composition of materials used by him. On the other hand the Parylene-C (polychloro-p-xylylene) a member of the poly-paraxylylene family of polymers, which is colourless, transparent, flexible, strong, highly conformal and its method of application causes minimal stress to textiles has been reported to be helpful in the case of highly degraded silk artifacts which are too weak to withstand stitching, this treatment seems to be appropriate. Parylene is unique in that it is reported to provide a protective sheath for each fiber in the fabric. In addition, the gas phase deposition of it produces a thinner and more highly conformal coating than can be achieved by liquid-based consolidation materials. It is an irreversible process, this should be used with caution, if nothing else works as a last resort. It does protect silk fragments from visible light.

Experiments conducted by (Karsten and others 2005) show that the peel strength of fabric specimens adhered with Lascaux 360/498 HV and prepared using acetone, IMS, and heat reactivation time, pressure and temperature was Acetone reactivation gave stronger bond than IMS or heat at constant time an pressure. IMS produced stronger bonds than heat at times over 5 minutes. Increasing reactivation time, pressure or temperature increased the peel strength. If levels were too high, the bond was very strong and adhesive was transferred to the artifact fabric peeling. This study has shown that conservators can manipulate these to achieve the bonds with it that range from very weak to very strong. Further success of this with actual practice on textiles would be interesting for the guidance of conservators.

**4. RESTORATION:-**

Any attempt to complete an old piece must not adversely affect it's original qualities. In India sewing to a backing material which has been dyed to blend with the missing part keeping in mind the background of the textile to which the backing should match so that the lost parts and the lacunae becomes less conspicuous or if the damages are minute these could be darned with a matching thread. Only a fine quality cloth backing of appropriate fineness is chosen for the new support and coarser materials should not be used as it may inflict further damage to the original. An important factor is the choice of materials-fabrics, threads, adhesives and consolidation process to give aesthetic support without future risk of adverse physical and chemical reactions with the original and ensure future stability for as long as possible. (Plate 33 & 34) The digital aspect of inkjet printing is being experimented further to create lost designs of old textiles to assist the restorers.

## 5. PREVENTIVE CONSERVATION:-

Preventive measures, if adopted as a policy by the Curators ,would go a long way to keep the textiles for a long time to be enjoyed by one and all. The quantum of work involved for preserving the textiles in totality is quite large and the measures to keep them in good state of preservation are still disproportionate to our actual needs. Moreover the entire collection of textiles would need these measures to be adopted irrespective of their conservation status. In this connection it should be ensured that the treated textiles also need the same preventive care as the whole collection otherwise the time and money which has been spent on them would go waste. We can provide preventive care to the entire collection of textiles and deter the decay. All of us know that environment plays a vivid role in the decay of textiles which has resulted into their scanty number available today in a museum. Most of the chemical reactions get accelerated in the presence of high RH and temperature. This points to the evaluation of the climatic conditions in a Building housing the collection. Round the clock control of these factors is necessary but various institutions have their own reservation in this regard. Some museums lament about funds, others lament about staff and some of them lament due to security reasons. Many institutions go on acquiring artifacts without adequate storage facility, dump them wherever they can make shift arrangements to keep them, others do not have adequate conservation and curatorial staff to maintain their vast collection. I sometimes wonder whether we can manage the show well or are we mismanaging the National assets?

Indecently we have to maintain a round the clock RH at 50% and a temperature range of 20 to 22 degrees Celsius in summers and 18 to 20 degrees Celsius in winters keeping the comforts of our visitors as well as to keep our prized possessions intact for research, study, interpret, disseminate knowledge and enjoy. Many Curators presume that no damage can happen to the textiles while on display, during storage and handling them, though the reality is not so. The various activities in a museum should keep in mind the conservation aspect in all the activities connected with the Curatorial duties/responsibilities as a collective endeavor. For different size and type of textiles proper planning of the storage, what procedures of display can harm the textiles and proper planning of their packing and transportation has to be mastered to reduce the damage to a bare minimum (Bisht, A.S. in, TRIRATNA Vol. II 2003). We should use acid–free tissue paper for packing and also use a acid free mount board box or a Polypropylene board box.

As regards control of environment is concerned what is first needed is the measurement of environmental parameters so that one knows when to humidify and when to dehumidify. A product named 'Art Sorb' of M/S Fuji Davision Chemical Ltd., Japan can be used to restrict the fluctuations of climate inside the building. Light levels also need to be monitored and controlled as per international standards. Good housekeeping, inspection of collections and meticulous cleaning use of tested materials for painting the showcases(sulphur free), polyester or biaxially oriented vinylon film instead of polythene for wrapping, acid free tissue for wrapping them or interleaving them or unbleached cotton cloth after removal of starch from them would go a long way to save textiles from decay. Ageless Z which can maintain low oxygen atmosphere in a sealed show case or storage space. These can check the growth of the bio–deterioration from textiles and are environment friendly. Textiles should be frequently rotated while on display to avoid damage by high intensity of light radiations ,avoid any undue strains on them due to gravity/weight. It is also advisable to keep light off and to switch on the lights only at the time of their viewing. Lights in the storage areas should be kept shut to keep them in dark and electric switch should be out side the stores. But this would go a long way to save the textiles provided the Curators inspect their collection at fixed intervals. There should also be adequate arrangements for fire fighting with Halon gas Bromo chloro difluoro methane ($CBrClF_2$) with smoke sensors as is available in the National Museum, New Delhi.

It should also be ensured that the Museum building is earthquake resistant and artifacts are well secured by designing earthquake resistant show cases. Assessment of existing buildings to be made by experts in the field and if found deficient, upgrading the strength by appropriate measures such as essential seismic strengthening of various elements to be done without waiting for an earthquake to happen. Those institutions having no such facilities to monitor the climate inside their premises should take the help of a trained and experienced Conservation Consultant.

Reviews in Conservation, IIC (2000) cited in the bibliography has reviewed the aspect of wet cleaning of historic textiles: surfactants and other wash bath additives. This is a thorough review of the aspect. However, only one paper from India has been included in the bibliography/references at the end of the review, probably due to lack of access to the material on the subject being published in India. In conclusion, the author hopes "that the above review shows importance of studying the 'industrial' literature, of allowing enough time for a thorough conservation related 'critical' adaptations and of being sufficiently fast in following initiatives towards new research". Some body from India has to volunteer to do the job of abstracting the various publications for AATA which are being published here. Many Conservators and Librarians who have been doing this work voluntarily until the end of the last century have retired now. I being one of them would request the people who are still in service to keep it going. Some times it is also expected from the Conservator that the final mounting method used by him/her should bear the stress and strain of the probable damage at the time of its actual exhibition being put on show. This can never be guaranteed that these would not get damaged even if mishandled. I think it is too much to expect from any Conservator.

Another branch of textile conservation which is getting into limelight is the conservation of Furniture and upholstery abroad and it would get boost in India also since many old palaces of erstwhile princely states have in their possession this category of antique furniture. Besides the houses of Governors of various states and of the President of India have this Victorian furniture. It would be recalled here that a large majority of these have been the one time residences of the various Viceroys and others during the British Raj before 1947. Folding of textiles to be avoided as it would weaken them at the point of folding. Keeping in bundles to be discarded especially of textiles having Zari. Iron clips etc. are not to be used with textiles as it would produce rust stain. Special storage for individual textile according to its structure has to be planed to restrict their damage as stated earlier in this book. The textiles are very sensitive works of art and get easily damaged with a little carelessness in the stores, display and transportation for exhibitions abroad. In a flash back I remember a large size tent used at the time of showing hunting adventures by Rajas and Maharajas in India was to go for an exhibition abroad and a committee of Conservation experts felt that the tent should not travel abroad because of the fact that it was too big in size and, therefore, did not approve its individual parts be dismantled and reassembled two times on each occasion when ever sent abroad for an exhibition.

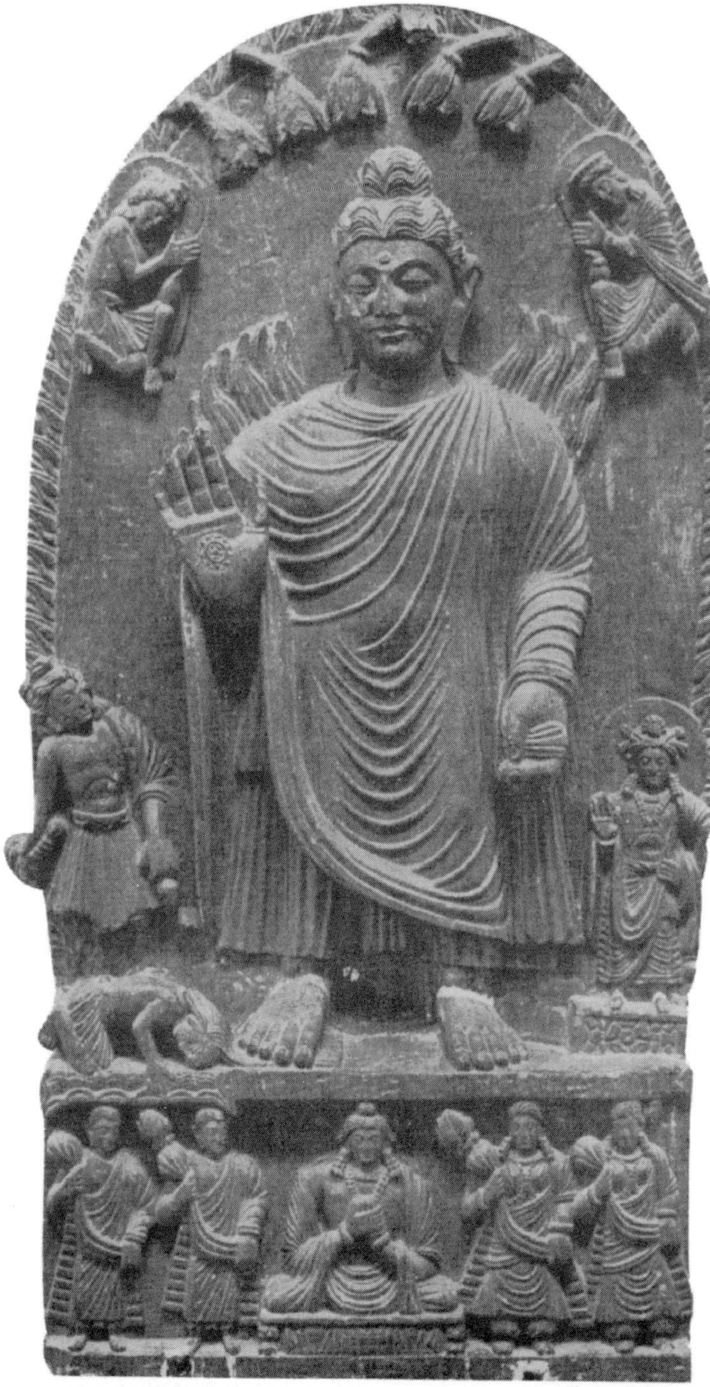

Pl. 1. Schist image showing folds of drapery 2nd-5th century AD Afghanistan

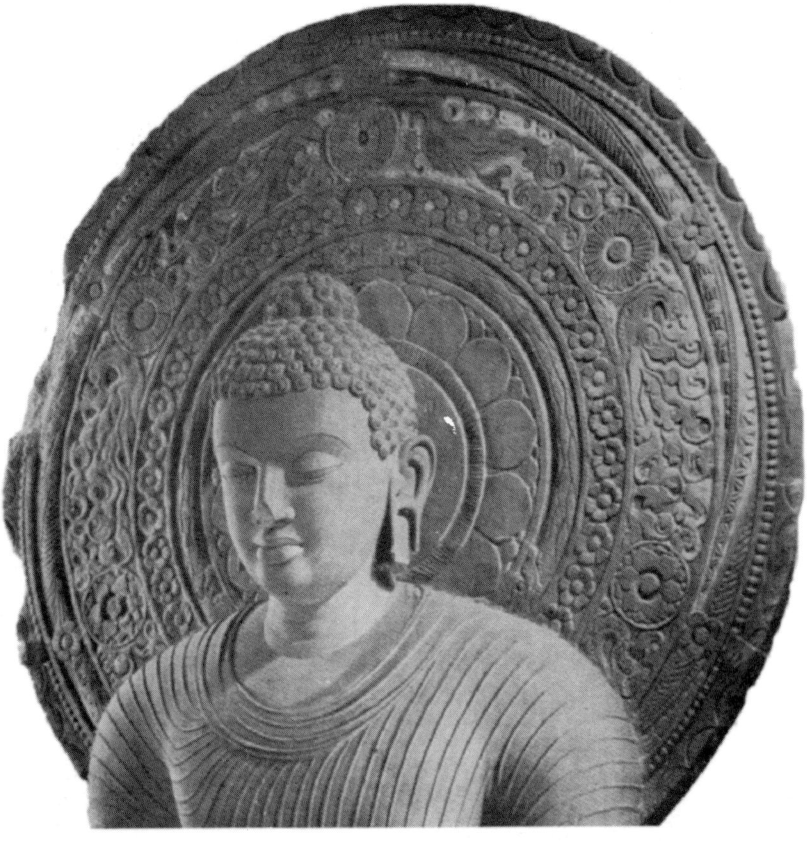

Pl. 2. Sand stone image showing folds of drapery of Gupta period India

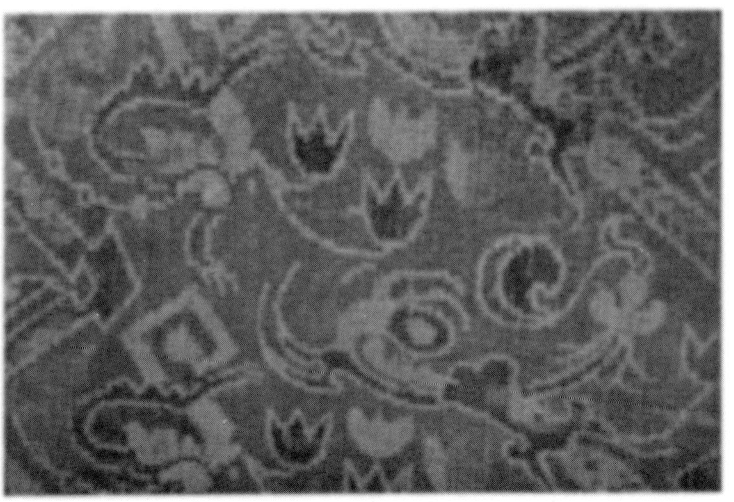

Pl. 3. Central Asian Textile

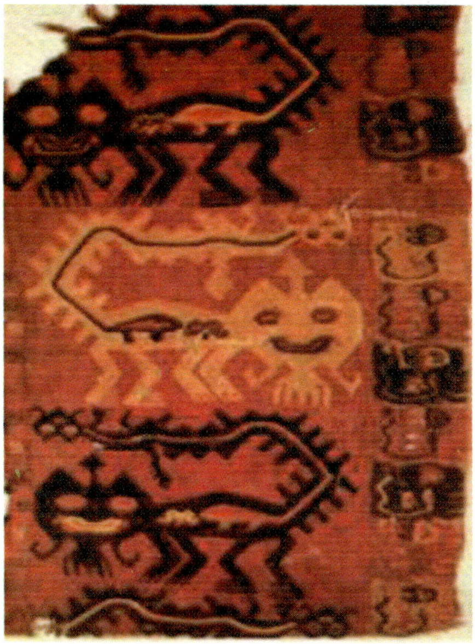

Pl. 4. Coptic textile South. America

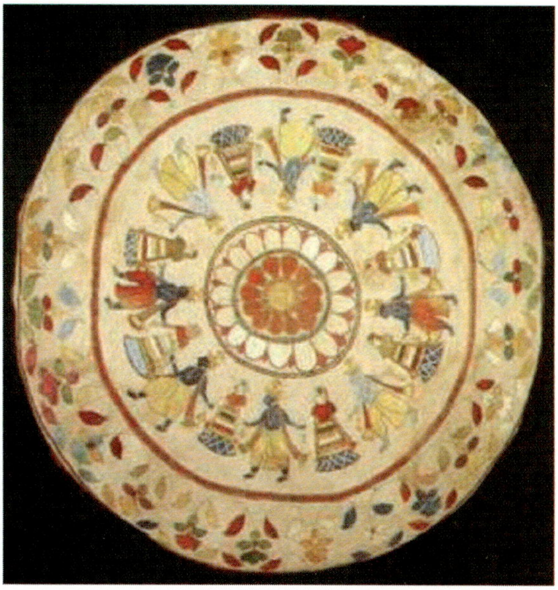

Pl. 5.Embroideroied Rumal, Raslila Chamba

Pl. 6. Pochampalli Blouse piece

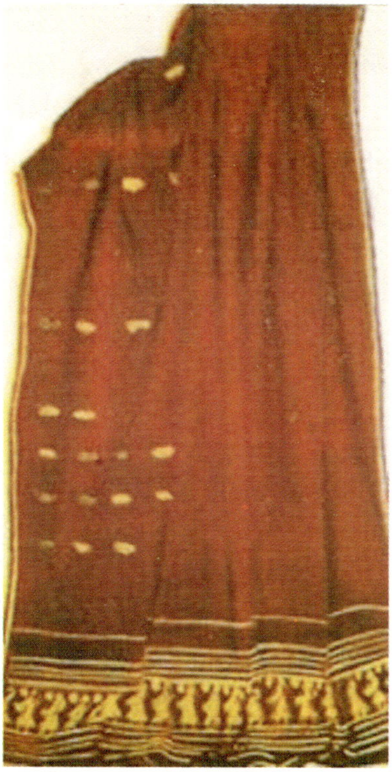

Pl. 7. Gollabhama Saree

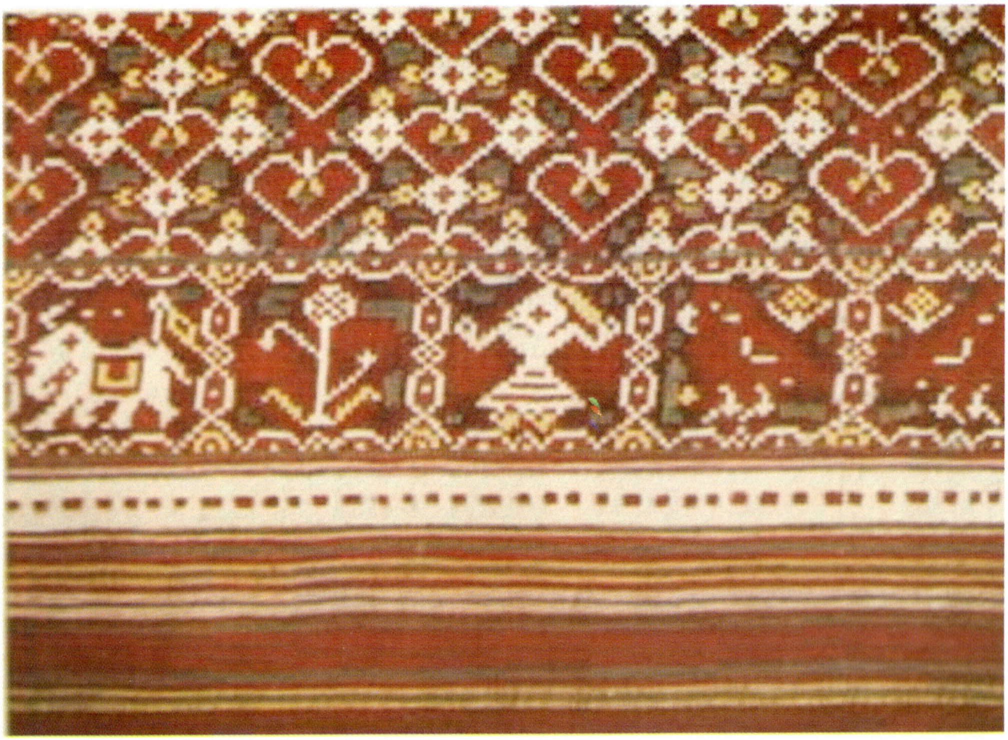

Pl. 9. Patola Saree from Gujarat

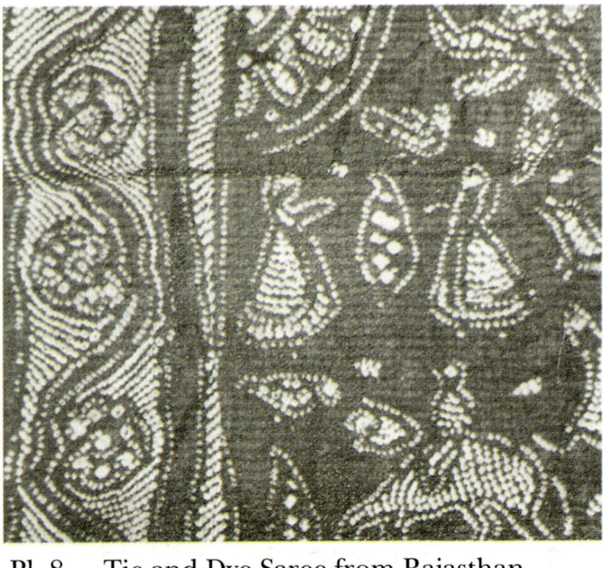

Pl. 8. Tie and Dye Saree from Rajasthan

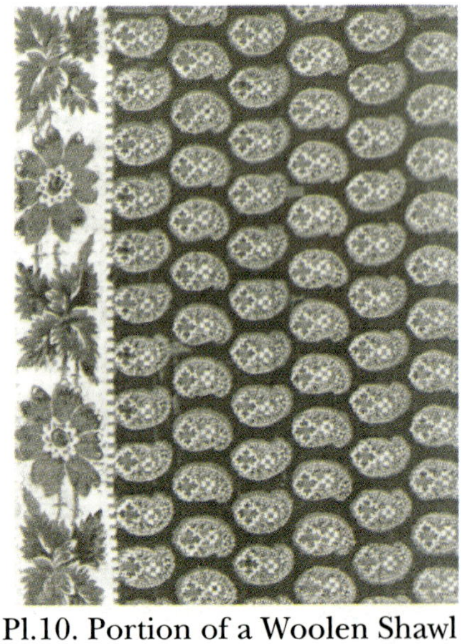

Pl.10. Portion of a Woolen Shawl

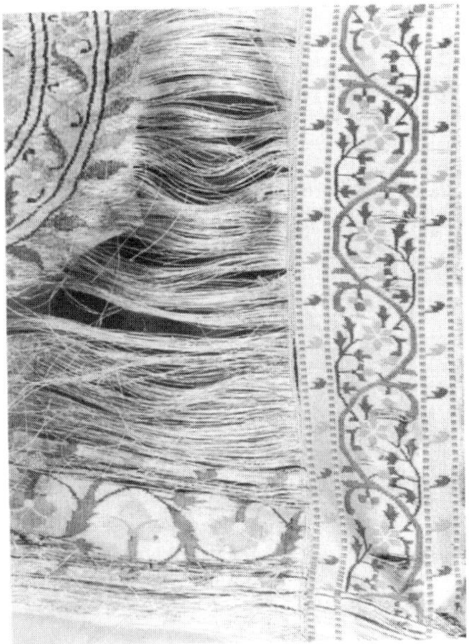

Pl. 11. Brocaded Saree from Benaras badly damaged due to friction of metallic threads with silk threads

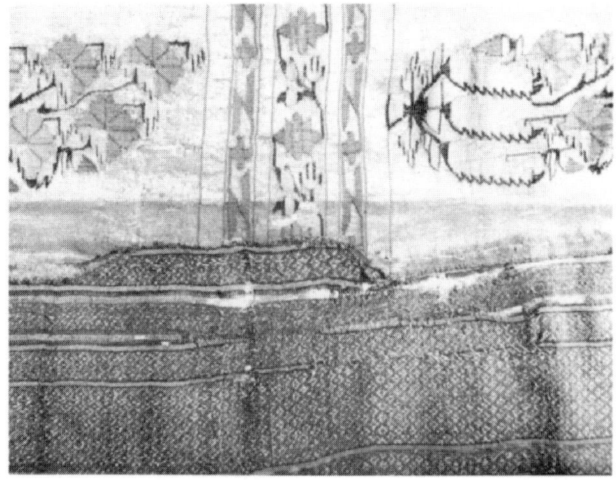

Pl. 12. Zari Border of a Saree dislocated due to loosening of stitches

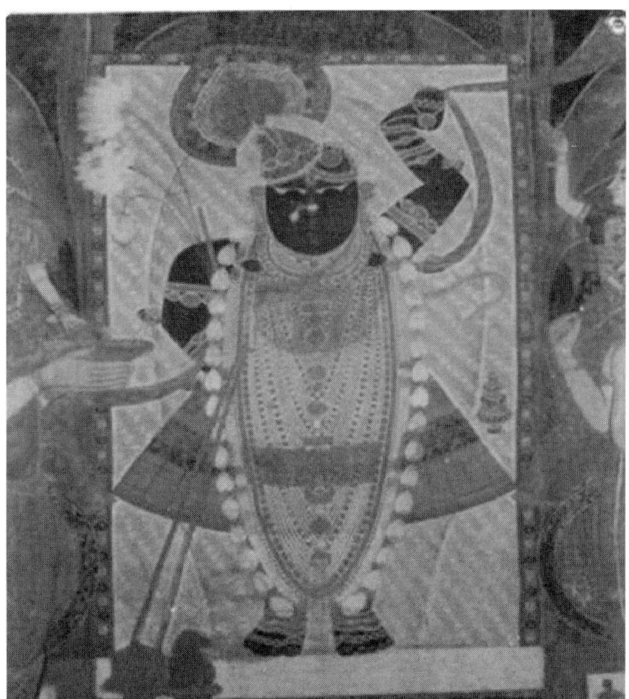

Pl. 13. Pichwai from Rajasthan before treatment

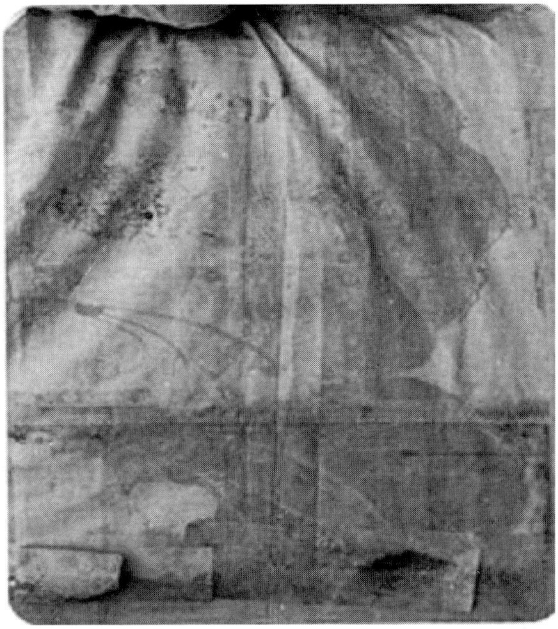

Pl. 14. Pichwai showing charring at the back due to use of acidic pigments

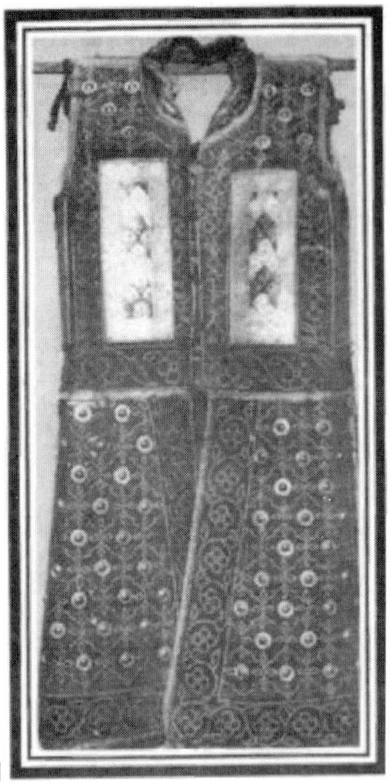

Pl. 15. War coat Mughal before restoration–the textile portion is badly damaged

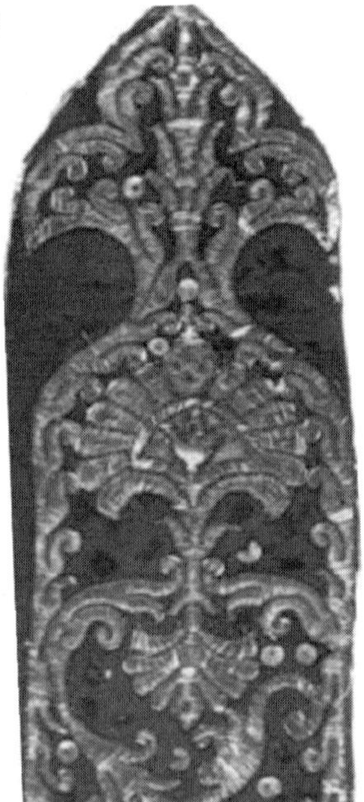

Pl. 16. Brocade Belt having tarnished Zari

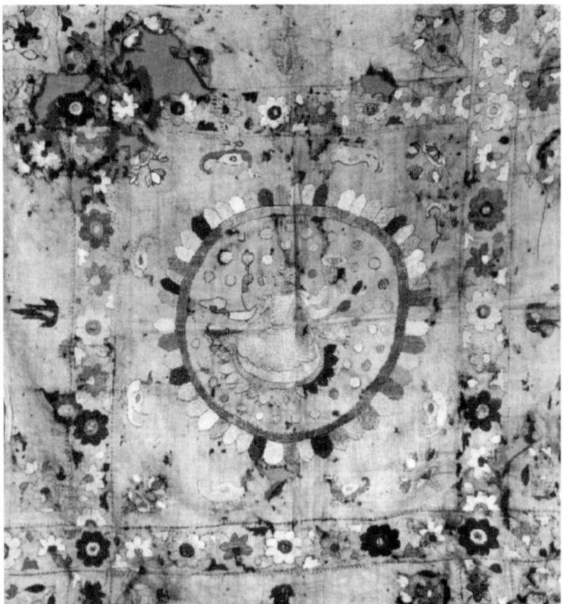

Pl. 17. Chamba Rumal in bad condition

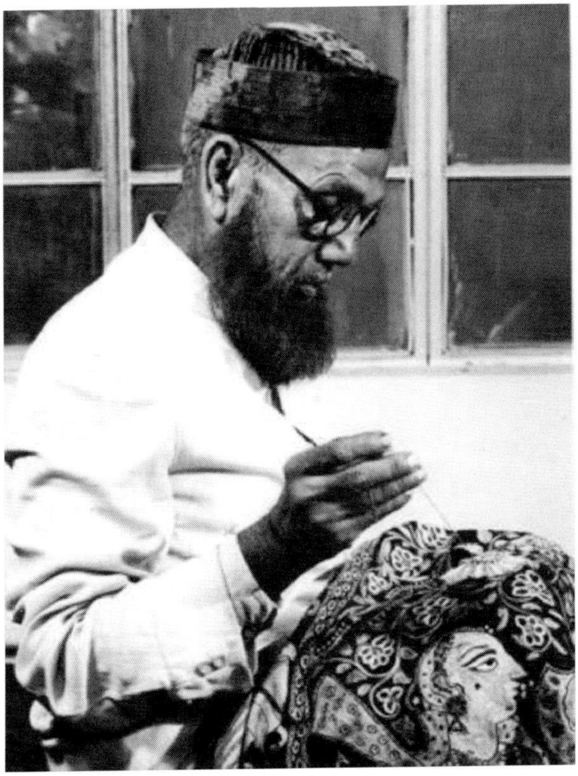

Pl. 18. Traditional method of restoration

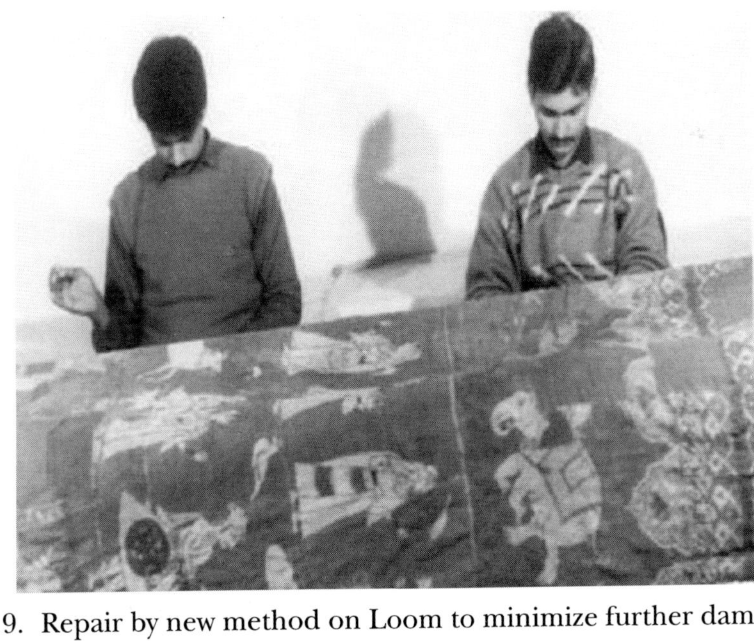

Pl. 19. Repair by new method on Loom to minimize further damage

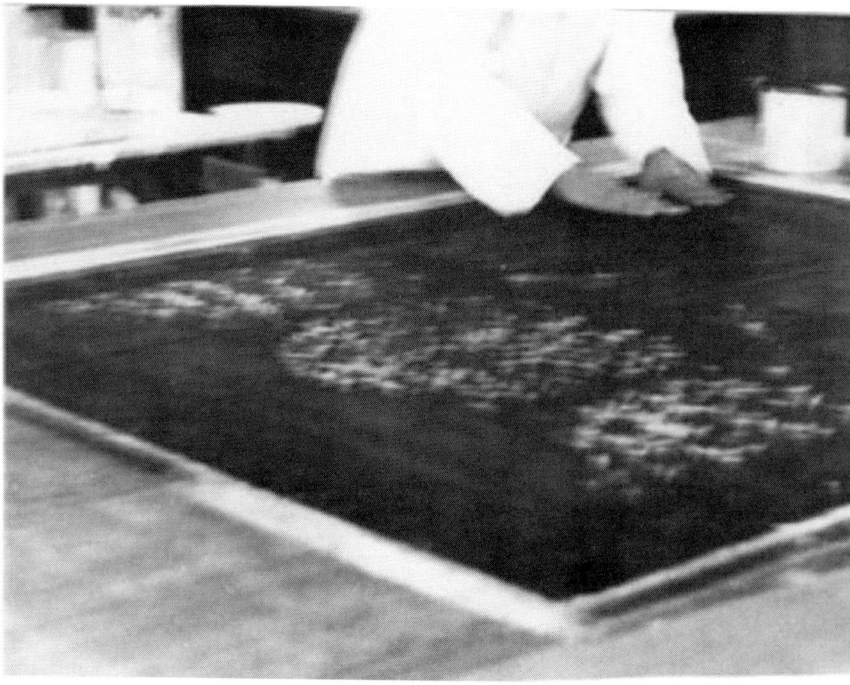

Pl. 20. Neutralization of acidity in textiles by washing

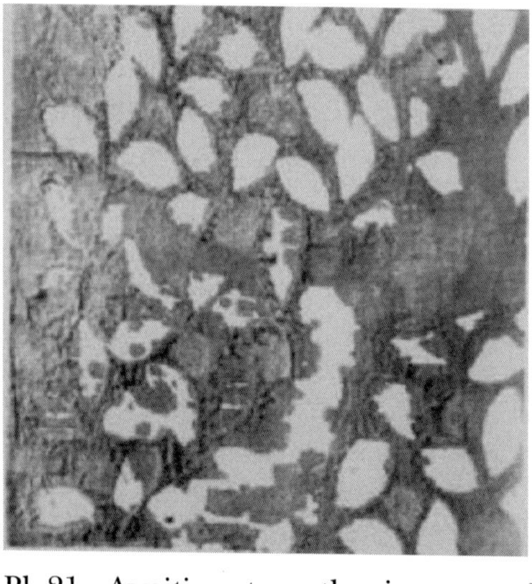

Pl. 21. Awaiting strengthening

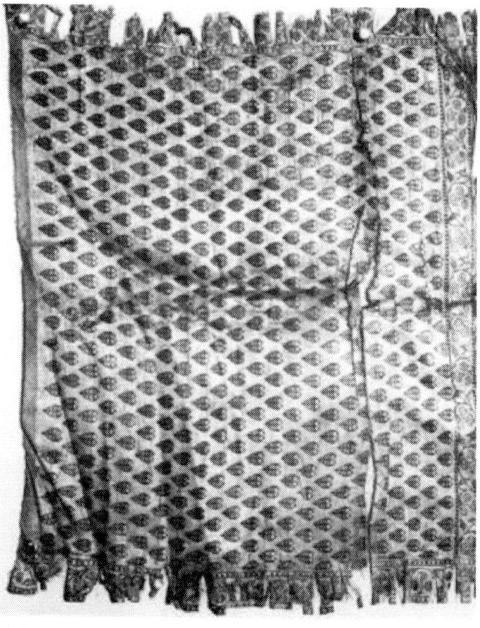

Pl. 22. Brocaded Textile before restoration

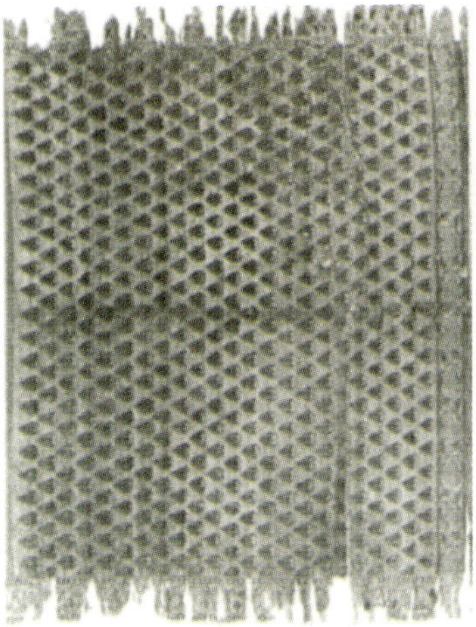

Pl. 23. Brocaded Textile after washing.

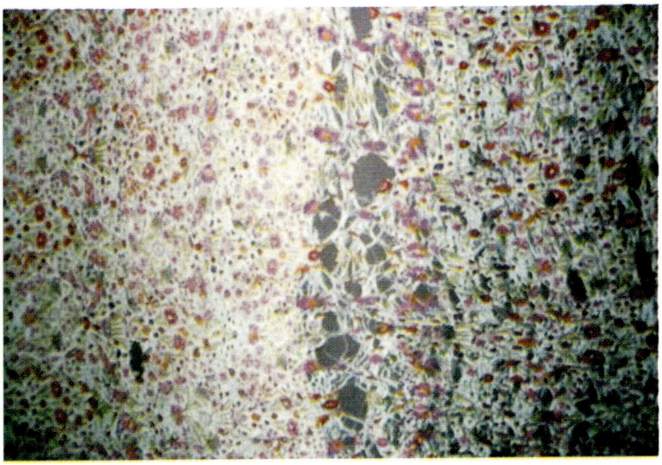

Pl. 24. Shawl - silk thread of warp is damaged due to its acidic nature and can not hold the weft .

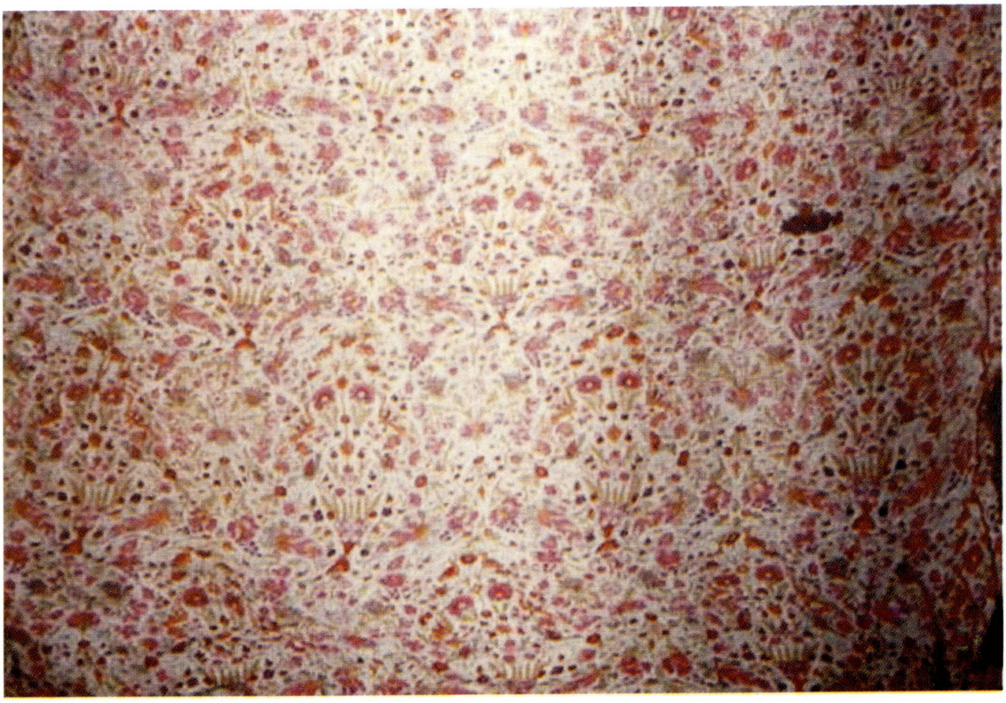

Pl. 25. Shawl after giving support of a similar material with needle and thread.

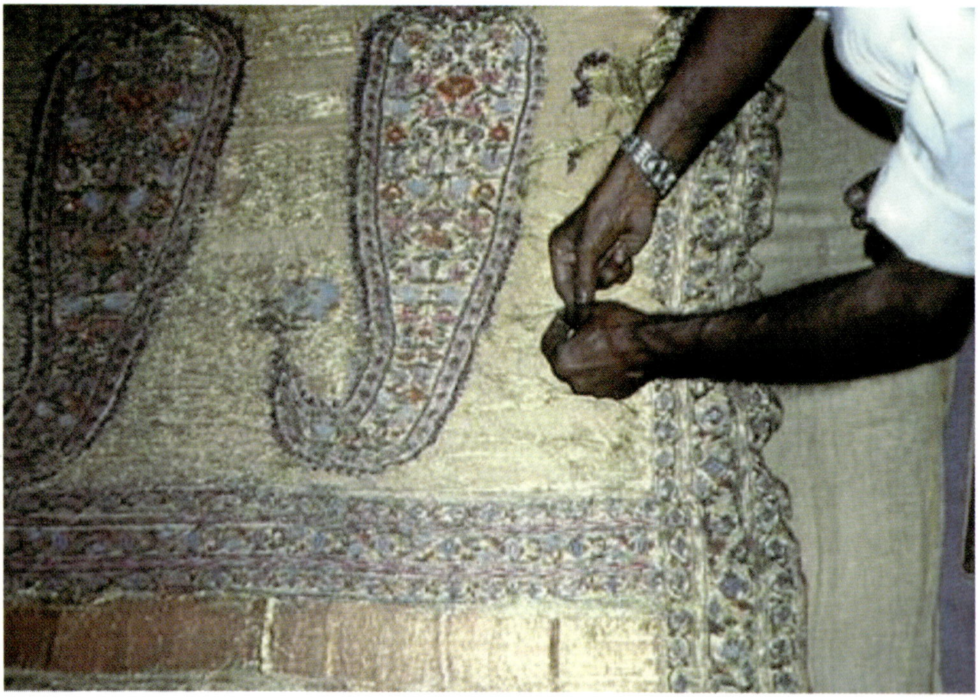

Pl. 26. Saree from Benaras highly damaged is seen during restoration.

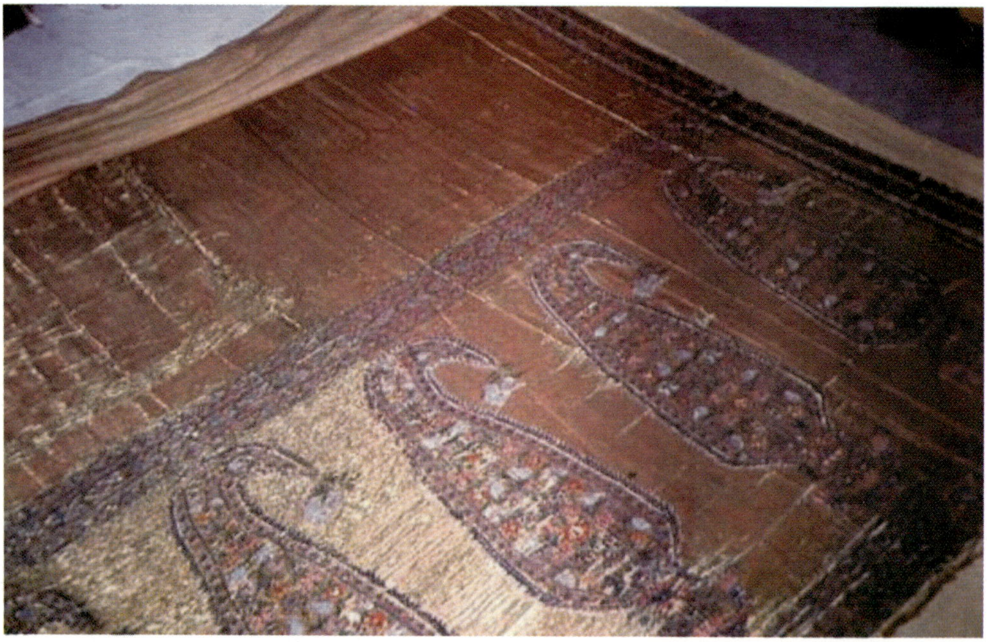

Pl. 27. Saree from Benaras after restoration by traditional method.

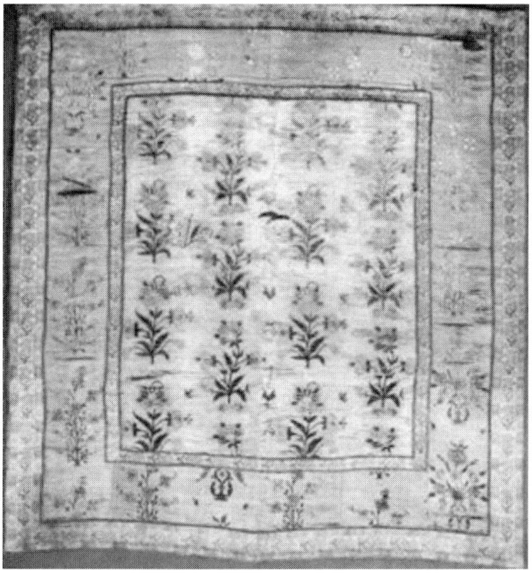

Pl.28.Prayer Carpet before restoration

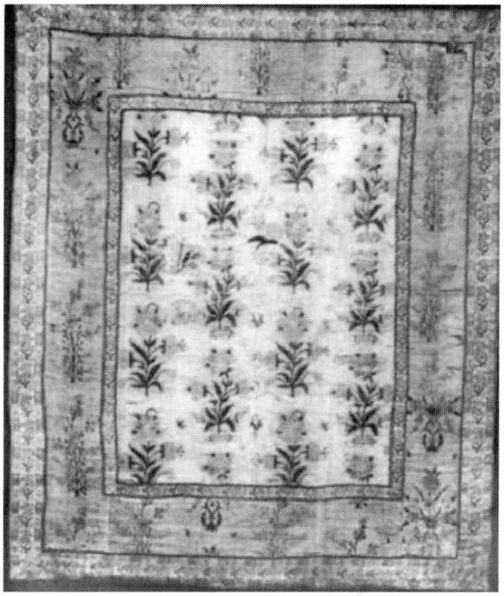

Pl. 29. Prayer Carpet after restoration by giving a new backing by needle and thread

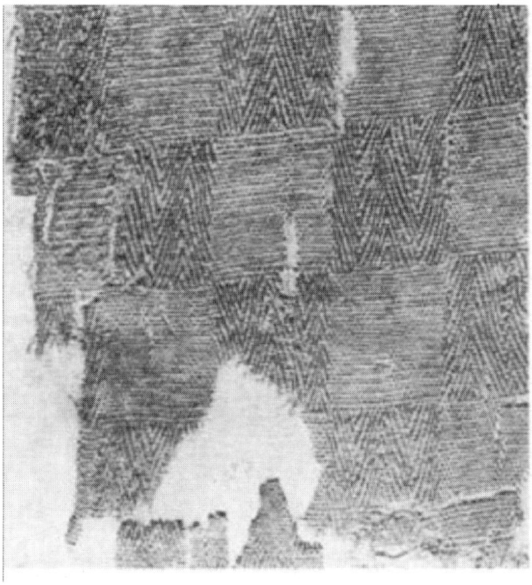

Pl. 30. Compatible Backing provided to a patterned silk fragment from central Asia by a water based adhesive

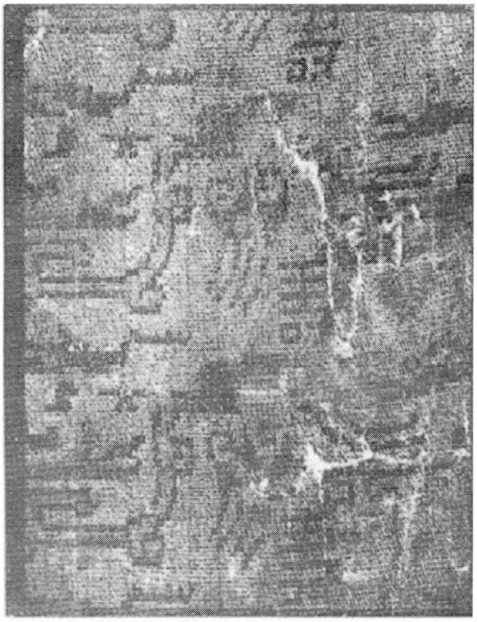

Pl. 32. A polychrome figured silk Central Asian from Lou-lan strengthened with fresh support using water based adhesive

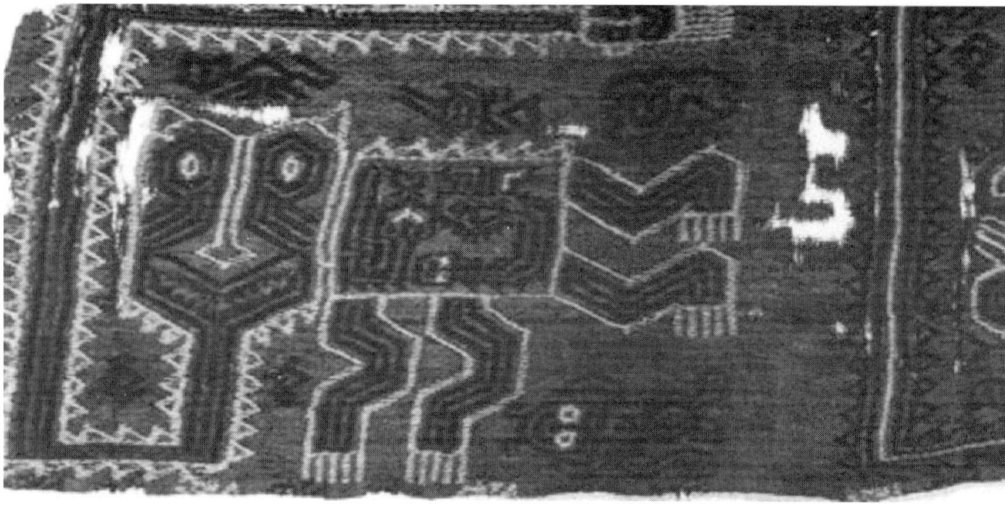

Pl. 31. Pre-Columbian textile from south America damaged

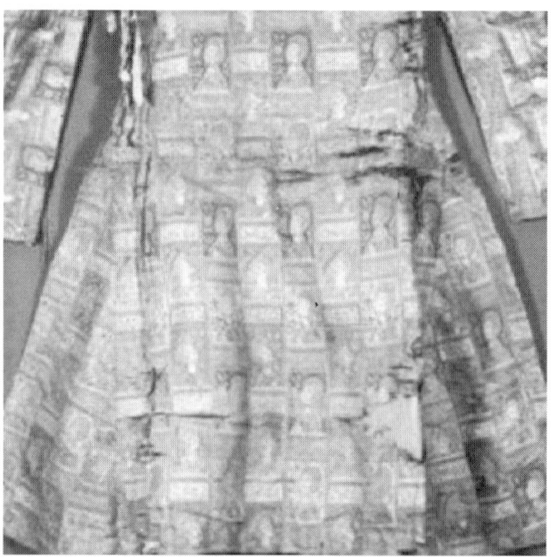

Pl. 33. Choga before restoration

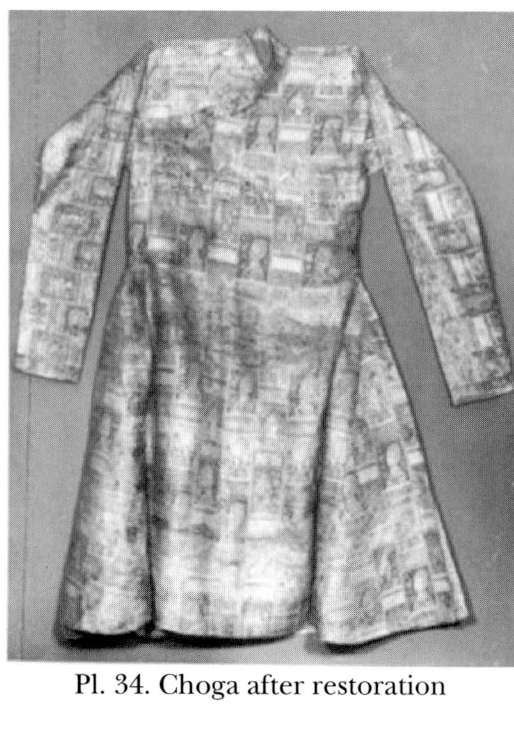

Pl. 34. Choga after restoration

# PART II

# CONSERVATION OF BONE AND IVORY

## CHAPTER VI

# INTRODUCTION

Ivory and bone have played special role as an attractive material from times of Prehistoric period and ancient times on up to period of modern arts and crafts. Although a great deal of Indian secular art was produced, it was essentially made of perishable material and, therefore, has not survived with the time. We have a very scanty surviving example of this great tradition of Ivory and bone due to its easily degradable material. These two materials are very similar in appearance and chemical formula, yet they are different in proportions of their compositional elements and their clearly defined physical microstructure under high magnification. With the scarcity of ivory today and due to ecological reasons people have no alternative but to use vegetable or synthetic materials or bone to cope with the demand for ivory for decorative art and crafts. Webster's Dictionary describes ivory as "The hard, smooth, yellowish dentine forming the main part of the tusks of elephant. A similar substance forming the tusks or teeth of certain other animals, such as the walrus and hippopotamus." They are considered ivory-like materials and differ primarily because they are harder and more brittle than true ivory. The Random House College Dictionary describes a vegetable ivory called, "ivory nut", a South American low palm tree nut, "Phytelephas macrocarpa", which yields a ivory like substance. Other palm trees nuts have similar characteristics. Reader's Digest Great Dictionary defines ivory as "a hard creamy-white substance composing the main part of the tusks of an elephant, walrus or narwhale." and bone as "any of the pieces of hard, whitish tissue making up the skeleton in vertebrates" usually bone of a cattle or oxen and human bones are used as substitutes for ivory.

Ivory tends to yellow with age and takes on a mellow brownish-yellow patina. In strict terms, true ivory comes from the tusks i e. the upper teeth of elephants. This includes both African and Asian species and their prehistoric ancestor, the mammoth Tusks of an African elephant are about 9 to 10 feet long and 160 lbs in weight (Plate 35). The tusks of an Indian elephant are about 6- 8 feet long and up to 90 lbs in weight (Plate 36). Recovery of bone or ivory from the excavations has helped in dating the site and also to know whether it has come from marine environment or simply the underground environment. The excavations at Mohenjodaro, plaque showing a male figure, Ivory (Plate 37) and many other examples of day to day use especially the lathe turned baton, Harappa, Comb with dot-in-circle motif, Ivory (Plate 38) and many other Indus valley sites such as Lothal, Rupar followed by the historic sites such as Taxila, Nagda. Prabhash, Mathura, Patna, Ahichhatra, Malwa, Ter, Bhokardan, Hastinapur, Jhusi, Dharnikota, Begram, Sisupalgarh, Khotan and followed by Kashmir, Orrisa, Eastern India, Deccan & Mysore have been reported including decorative carvings from all over India of ivory and bone objects. Two elephant tusks reported and found at Mohenjodaro along with nine Skeletons 'buried at the same time' (E. Mackay) feels that these belong to one family which was fleeing the place along with their priced possessions due to some natural calamity or due to some other reason.

National Museum, New Delhi has a very pride historical possession of the sacred relics (Plate 39) of Buddha the Great (5th-4th cent. B.C.) in its collection given by the Archaeological Survey of India as a long term loan which were unearthed from Piprehwa, Distt. Basti U.P. in the two Steatite Casket (Plate 40). A 11th cent. Copper plate inscription which was reportedly (Dwivedi 1976) unearthed from a mound in undivided Bengal at Bhatera village near Syhetis, mentioning that an ivory carver was attached to a Shiva temple. This makes it apparent that the trade of ivory was held in high respect and that the objects of ivory were used even in a temple. Similarly Orissa, according to an inscription datable to third quarter of $10^{th}$ cent. AD, was also famous for ivory *'hastidanta'* and ivory products from ancient times.

## 1. TRADITION OF CARVING

Ivory carving is one of the most ancient crafts of India. This is one of India's oldest and precious crafts. Indian ivories are known to have been exported abroad as far back as Roman times. Satavahanas, whose empire is reported to have flourished from 1st cent. B.C. to the early 3rd century A.D. in India giving a great thrust to international trade. Some references are available of a similar statuette found in Ter that has the same hole, and with another one found in Bhokardan. The affinity with the latter is particularly evident, so much so that it is thus thought that both were made in the same workshop. The notable quantity of objects in ivory, even unfinished are mentioned to have been found during excavations of Pompeii (79 AD.) and one can easily believe that Bhokardan was an import center for ivory-working. One can therefore, is compelled to think that our statutte did not reach Italy by chance but rather may have been brought as a souvenir directly from its place of production by some merchant from Pompeii who had been there. There has been an intense trading activity reported especially between India, China and Italy via the fabled Silk Route during Roman times as one finds many objects of artistic importance of India in Italy and vice versa as would be seen from the great similarity between the ivory statues from Pompeii, Italy (Plate 41) and Ter, India, (Plate

42) as reported in Ancient Rome and India- edited Rosa Maria Cimino (1994).

In medieval times, two major ivory carving traditions emerged. In the south, emphasis was laid on the making of sacred images carved in the round. Under Mogul influence in the north, a sophisticated and stylized form evolved using filigree jali work and low relief in fine floral and geometrical designs. Ivory is a precious material and a difficult one to carve; yet the Indian craftsmen have mastered this art from ancient times. Export of these ivory carved items continued from the Roman times. The important centers for ivory carving in India were Trivandrum in Kerala, Mysore and Bangalore in Karnataka, Delhi, Jaipur and Jodhpur in Rajasthan, Varanasi in Uttar Pradesh, Amritsar in Punjab, Murshidabad in West Bengal, Puri in Orissa and Kerala. Ivory carving in India has been an extremely popular craft since ages. Among the legendary merchandise that made India fabulous through the then known world was ivory, like frankincense and muslin. The Vedic text includes it amongst the noblest of crafts. There are references in Vedic literature of (*hastin)* elephants. Rig veda is reported to have a mention of a dice of ivory. This has been reported (Dwivedi 1976) as the earliest reference of ivory. The Ramayana has many references in its Ayodhya kanda, Aranya kanda, Kiskindha kanda and Sundara kanda, by which we know about the use of ivory and bone in that era. We also find many references of ivory and bone in Mahabharata, Buddhist Vinaya texts, Buddhist jatakas, Arthasastra, Silappadhikaram, Vishnudharmottra Purana and many other scriptures Indian as well as foreign. down the centuries up to modern times. In the Indus valley civilization (2500 and 1750 B C ) excavations spread over a large part of India we find many mentions showing use of bone and ivory for artifacts and utilitarian objects prominent among these are Plaque showing standing Male figure, Animal headed hairpin, Handle of ivory, Lathe turning baton from Mohenjodarȯ, Comb with dot-in-circle motif, Peg or Terminal, from Harappa, and Measuring Scale, Rods and points etc. of Ivory from

Lothal besides objects like tools and implements made of bone and ivory from similar sites of Indus culture. Use of both ivory and bone is quite evident from these sites.

According to history, King Solomon acquired Indian Ivory in 10th Century B.C, and King Darius used ivory decorations in his palace in 6th century B.C. The tradition of ivory and bone carving in India has been going on from the historic Period at various centers spread through out the length and breadth of the country. A 18th century carved ivory chair was given to Warren Hastings, the first British Governor-General of India, by Mani Begum of Murshidabad as seen in the (Plate 43) which show that ivory craft in India besides the images Lord Ram, Sita and Lakshman Set (Plate 44) 20th. cent. from Jaipur made by Gori the Craftsman who is still living and had an Exhibition of his works in Italy.

Ivory carving in Delhi walled city, was being practiced since many centuries now. It flourished during the Moguls through the ivory carvers. In Jaipur bangles are reported being made from the cylindrical part of the elephant tusks. Up to 1950's bangles and statues were being made from the tusks at Jaipur and Udaipur. The trade was dominated by the Kumawats (Masons) in Rajasthan having a good status in the society. The Ivory Carvers in Karnataka were doing the wood carving before they switched over to ivory. The Carvers of Karnataka were from the community of *Vishwakarmas* as they could carve ivory with the same tools as were being used by them for the sandal and rosewood carvings. In Kerala ivory carving has been a tradition for the *Achary* community as they found it good medium for making ivory statues of Gods and Goddesses. The Ivory Carvers of Orissa were also doing carving in stone and wood. They were from the *Mahapatraa* and *Maharana* cast who claim to be descendents of artisans who were engaged in Lord *Jagannath* Temple in the past.

These cavers used similar tools for carving of ivory as used for stone and wood carving by their ancestors In Murshidabad the ivory carving has been a traditional craft and carvers were called as *Bhaskar.* They got full support from their rulers and developed proficiency in this art of ivory carving. It was a State capital in West Bengal during the Mogul Rule and the artisans made many artifacts for the prince and princess. The carving of ivory in Varanasi specialized in making ivory *Jalis* of intricate designs for boxes, table lamps and other items of decorative nature and were also called *Viswakarmas* (among Hindus) and also the Muslims as ivory carvers of Varanasi. This trade had the support and was patronized by the then rulers. The Ivory carvers of Bengal, Jaipur and Delhi produced objects such as the ambari hathi or processional elephant, models of bullock carts, caskets, book covers, sandals, palanquins and frames for the European market. In Orissa, there has been a tradition of offering ivory inlaid furniture to the temple of Puri. Miniature shrines with delicate pillars and intricate low relief floral work, caskets depicting scenes from myths and legends, and images of gods and goddesses including Christian icons and symbols has been a tradition in Kerala and Karnataka. The work on the doors of the Amer palace in Jaipur and the exquisite in-lay in the Mysore palace doors and the Golden Temple at Amritsar proclaim the architectural decoration with Ivory.

## 2. LITERARY EVIDENCES:

The ancient belief that Lord Indra collected the bones of hermits especially from the Dadhichi's ashram to prepare a *Vajra* from the bones to be given to Lord Indra to fight the Demons. This suggests the use of ivory and bone implements to be used in wars. It is also a popular belief that about 20,000 BC people in eastern Europe used mammoth bones to make their tents to live since they made their tents from animal skins stretched over a frame made of wood or animal bones. The word ivory is derived from the Latin word *ebur.* The term "Ivory" though loosely applied to the tooth structure of the elephant are strictly speaking confined to the "dentine present only in the tusks of the elephant". Teeth of Walrus, hippopotamus, whale and some other animals are also named by some scholars as ivory. (Agarwal 1977) reported that ivory from elephant tusks is most common, but walrus ivory from the far north of Europe was esteemed in Mughal periods in north India and was imported for hilts of swords and daggers. Bone was also used for this purpose. In Tibet, finely carved bone ornaments, were used by religious functionaries for special ceremonies. Sanskrit word *"Ibha"* (Elephant) and *"Ibha danta"* (Elephant tusk) are also mentioned in ancient Indian literature. Ivory's appeal to the upper-classes as a symbol of affluence and its timeless style has lured people to the tusks since as far back as the ancient Egyptians around the year 3000 BC.

Since the Egyptians, every civilization with a significant upper class population has sought ivory and been willing to pay a premium price for it. The front gate of the Kabul Museum, Afghanistan is shown here as it was in 1990. (Plate 45) is of the photo taken by my team and photo in (Plate 46) is down loaded by from internet. This is the height of what terrorism could stoop to and shows what the man made disasters could do to our cultural heritage. These photos of (Plate 47, 48, 49, 50, 51, 52, 53) were taken by my team while I was there. This ivory collection was not only the pride of Afghanistan but of the cultural ethos of the Great Kushan empire which extended and ruled this part of the globe at one time.

Its collection through the years was enriched by the efforts of the then authorities with the help of the various archaeological expeditions to Afghanistan and it stood as one of the greatest testimonies of antiquity that the world has inherited. Major part of this great collection was already shifted from the museum premises by the authorities, when I was in Kabul, to a safe place in view of the threat from the terrorist. Even then, I consider myself fortunate having examined this world famous collection as was where was before the actual loot of the artifacts of the Kabul Museum, Kabul about which no body is sure where it is now. It is believed that the Begram ivories in such a large number suggests that these were part of a trading collection as most of them were found in boxes as if stored in a shop or go downs. This is supported by people who have visited that country at a later date.

As per references, Kerala specialized in the carving of God and Goddesses images in Ivory. The carvings are in the round and are based on the different styles of the temple sculptures of the area. The master craftsmen of Kerala made many other figures with rhythmic and expressive stances. Mysore developed this craft under the patronage of the royal court. The artists prepared deities, carved bedposts and intricate inlay patterns for doors, windows and ceilings. In North India, ivory carving developed during the reign of the Mughals. Delhi and Lucknow were important centers noted for their floral motifs, geometrical patterns carved in low relief or worked in fine Jali work. Small items like caskets and pen cases were also produced. Delhi is also known for its ivory costume jewellery and ceilings. Tamilnadu the state with its profusion of temples with carvings could not but specialize in figures of gods and goddesses of superb workmanship. Scenes from Ramayana and other epic stories and statue of St. George on a giant Charger killing the dragon with his spear. Veneered ivory work from Vishakhapatanam, Rajasthan and Gujarat are important centers for ivory bangles for women. The lathe- worked ivory bangles are Lacquered in red and are given to the women folk during their marriage. Rajkot is famous for ivory combs. Amritsar in Punjab developed ivory carving during the Sikh rule. It is famous for table lamps, bracelets and chess sets in ivory. Varanasi also produced many designs based on local traditions, as it is a big pilgrimage center for the Hindus and Buddhists. West Bengal has its own style of carving based on local folk traditions. Intricately carved figures of elephants and Goddess *Durga* are the common items done here. Orissa also has an important tradition of ivory carving. Ancient temples and palaces here have ivory carved items like the *mithuna* figure, etc. Of late this craft alas is dying as the Indian Government has banned the elephant poaching and on ivory-working. This ofcourse was necessary to save our ecology. Hence the carvers are now turning onto other crafts particularly, bone-carving. This craft has been prevalent in India from ancient times.

The tribal are usually associated with this craft. The Himalayan tribals practice this craft for making ritual items. In Orissa, bone carvings of animals and *mithuna* figures are common. Carved combs of bones and horns are a specialty. The most important centers include Sarai Tarin in Uttar Pradesh, Cuttack and Parlakimedi in Orissa, Honawar in Karnataka and Trivandrum in Kerala. Decorative combs, buttons, flower vases, penholders, cutlery items, toys are some of the common items that are done in these places. The Horn combs prepared in India are still very popular throughout the world. In Cuttack horn and filigree work are combined to produce decorative jewels, bangles, etc. The craftsmen of Trivandrum are famous for making different kinds of crane birds in horn.

Since there is still considerable speculation about the origin of the Begram ivory and bone objects(Agrawal,V.S.1946-7) having a mention of two ivory objects called as Indian Ivory plaque showing Purna Ghata found at Kapisa, Afghanistan, and an Indian Ivory plaque showing winged lion found in Afghanistan which was shown in the Inter-Asian Exhibition of Art and Archaeology in The Central Asian Antiquities Museum, New Delhi from March 22 to April 6, 1947. The Begram excavation has yielded no definitive evidence of a workshop e.g. instruments, discarded worked ivory -the exact way in which the Begram objects were created remains a conjecture. However, certain technical aspects in the making of ivory and bone sculptures in general are known from archaeological findings, literary evidence and ethnoarchaeological studies of more modem ivory carvers and as indicated by several scholars, the instruments employed in the sculpting of ivory and bone have not undergone many changes since pre-historic times (Dwivedi 1976). Turning to the subject matter of the ivory and bone objects, as noted previously, it can be assigned to the general Central/South Asian sphere of influence. The topics are a common mix of realistic and mythological motifs found in the arts of *Gandhara, Mathura, Bactria* and neighboring regions in Central and South Asia. The majority of the central themes on the pieces are depictions of women, in single or multiple form, a motif very popular in the art of the Indian subcontinent. Architectural forms, too, compare favorably with the arts of India.

There are also subjects which suggest a blending of various art styles, a result of the cross-cultural tendencies of the *Kushan* period. Although a correlation between technique, style and/or subject matter might provide a basis on which to assign common origins for some of the pieces, no such clear connection arises. There is a slight correlation between technique and subject matter in some of the carvings, but it seems to provide no supportable link to a place of origin. According to (Hackin 1939), flat relief, is mainly used for floral and zoomorphic designs (Hackin). It is also on the flat relief pieces that red paint is used for the grounding. However, while this may be true for some objects discovered, it does not hold true for the other finds, among with which were several plaques depicting humans, executed in flat relief and showing traces of red paint. Even to the extent Hackin is correct that the flat relief plaques are carved with predominantly floral and faunal motifs, the exact same floral and zoomorphic designs are also present on plaques carved by a different technique. Lastly, it seems important here to touch upon the material aspects of the Begram objects. As noted previously, the Begram carvings consist of both bone and ivory, and the question here is whether there is a correlation between the material and the technique, style and/or subject matter. Technique of flat relief appears almost exclusively on bone. Both ivory and bone are used for the incised or engraved pieces and for pieces in light relief. However, only ivory is used for high relief or pieces in the round. These differences seem to indicate little more, however, than that the bone used in Begram pieces was not technically suitable for thick carving or carving in the round. In addition, bone seems to have been used almost solely, though with a few exceptions, for less important pieces of ensembles, while the main scenes were in ivory.

This is an unsurprising finding since ivory is virtually always more scarce and therefore, more valuable than bone. Cutler (1985:59-64), in a study of mainly Byzantine ivory art, also notes that in larger panels bone is mainly used for secondary elements such as floral and faunal motifs. In addition, Cutler makes the interesting observation that objects which were unique, that is, only one piece produced, had no bone elements and that bone appeared most frequently in pieces that were 'mass produced'. As will be discussed in the following sections, the presence of so many bone objects within the Begram hoard may likewise suggest that they may have been 'market' products rather than royal treasure. What remains is the conclusion that the Begram ivory and bone pieces were an amalgam of styles and techniques which were used simultaneously to create a heterogeneous collection of objects, the dating, origin and nature of which remain subject to other factors for elucidation. In some, and with few exceptions, there seem to be no direct correlations among technique and style, subject matter and/ or material. Above the confluence of the Ghorband and Panjsher Rivers near the village of Begram, some 40 miles north east of Kabul lies the ancient site of Begram on the silk route as a testimony of the great trade route showing the trade activities. When I was visiting the various Begram room in the Kabul Museum and was having a look at the ivory collections housed there in showcases and later viewing the various almirahas and boxes containing ivories it was an exiting scene for me seeing such a large collection at one place even though it was not the full collection. Alas! I was not destined to conserve them even though my report was with the UNESCO since what happened after 1990 is known to all. I retired from the National Museum, New Delhi in March 1991. There was a phone call, 2-3 months after from the UNESCO representative, at that time stationed in Pakistan, due to Taliban rule in Afghanistan and I referred her to see my report with them.

In medieval India ivory workers were active in the different parts of the country, and the ivory inlay doors of *Asaf-I-sarifin* Bijapur of A.D. 1580, represent a fine example of ivory work at the beginning of the Islamic rule in India. Skill of Indian craftsmen in ivory, in medieval times were Amritsar, Patiala, Delhi, Varanasi, Lucknow, Orissa, Murshidabad, Surat, Ahmedabad, Balsar, Satara, Vishagapatam, Vijaynagar, Karnataka and some towns of Kerala. Carved ivory fans from West Bengal; ivory bracelets from Jodhpur; veneered ivory work from Vishagapatam, carved combs from Rajkot, buttons, powder boxes, caskets and umbrella handles from Ahmedabad and Surat and bangles from Cuttak display fine workmanship. Images of mythological interest, scenes from contemporary life and objects of daily use like paper-cutters, comb, bangles and even toys are produced in various workshops of south India. Crafts made from shell, bone and horn were also used by people of medieval period. *Surmadanis,* cases for black antimony for eye decoration are made of camel bones; buffalo-horn is also used for combs, boxes, *hukka* mouth pieces, munals, pen-holders, ivory Bracelets from Pali in Marwar, Rajasthans and a large number of other objects of utility. This run-away market is not just for Oriental ivory, but almost as figures of 19th century and earlier European ivory has all but disappeared. The ivory market surged upward almost unnoticed by the general public. It has done what silver did in the early 1980's. Ivory specimens date back to the earliest dynasties of Egypt. A great wealth of ivory-carving has survived from early Christian times in the West and many fine works in ivory have also come down to us from remote civilizations in China and the Near East. Some pieces of this great Begram collection of a period datable to lst to the middle 3rd century

A.D., have been given on loan to the National Museum for display and placed at the disposal of the National Museum, New Delhi for permanent display. Ivory craftsmen of Gujarat made human figures as also statues of deities in excellent quality. Punjab's highly decorated elephants and figurines depicting characters from folk or heroic tales are superb. Uttar Pradesh is famous for its Hindu and Buddhist figures of deities, dancing poses and decorative plaques.

In transverse sections it shows lines of different colors proceeding in the arc of a circle. Ivory has a distinctive, "engine-turned" cellular appearance under magnification. The hard white substance composing the tusks of elephant is quite dense and the pores are close, compact and filled with a gelatinous solution which makes it easily amenable to the carver's skill. The solution contributes to the beautiful polish given to the objects produced from Ivory, being fibrous, it can not also be easily torn. When most people think of ivory, they think of elephants and their huge curving tusks. Most of the major museums in India have a magnificent collection of ivories especially in the museums of National importance, state museums, museums run by the trusts related to erstwhile princely states and many more including the National Museum, New Delhi. Those tusks are actually teeth, and that's what ivory is. Ivory, apart from elephant tusk is also obtained from other animals with large teeth, such as the walrus, hippopotamus, narwhal and sperm whale. In India mostly the ivory is the real ivory. As some of these animals, particularly elephants, are endangered species, it's now illegal to import/export most ivory. Since 1989, there has been a worldwide ban on any trade in elephant's ivory. Due to these regulations, the value of ivory carvings has tremendously increased. Ivory had been the most fascinating material to work for craftsman since the ages.

## 3. COLLECTION OF MAJOR MUSEUMS IN INDIA AND ABROAD:

The collection of the National Museum, New Delhi is vary varied which is housed in its various departments such as Gunpowder flask, Gun handle, Dagger, Elephant Goad, Spear, Sickle etc. in the Arms & Armor Gallery, Tanpura, Veena, Sur-Bahar, Sitar, Sarangi, Flute etc. in the Musical instruments gallery, Shringardan Paper Knives, Screen with Mughal Portraits, Chess Board, Chess men etc. in the Decorative art gallery. Walrus ivory handle, Fish plaque of Walrus ivory etc. in the Pre columbian and Western Art gallery and Playing cards, Ivory based painting, Painted ivory counters and dices, Painted ivory sculptures in the Miniature Gallery. Besides these, there are a number of ivory and bone artifacts in the collection of its various departments and are stored in the reserve collection of the individual departments. Most of the ivory objects are composite in nature along with other materials and are for decorative purposes such as along with silver, iron wood etc. Some of the ivory objects are simple and some are carved bedposts (Plate 54), the cross section of some genuine ivories showing the cracking pattern (Plate 55) and images of gods such as Lord Krishna (Plate 56) and Ganesha carved on a bedpost (Plate 57) besides many more examples of decorative ivory screen and decorative ivory spear etc. in the collection of the National Museum, New Delhi over the years acquired by its Art Purchase Committee till recently. The most interesting ivory pieces are the Begram ivories in our Sunga gallery on permanent loan from the National museum, Kabul.

The Salar Jung Museum, Hyderabad is a treasure house of art objects coming from different parts of the world including ivories. It has full tusks from China and Myanmar which are fully carved from Burma. One can see the development of this art in India even though the specimens are not of very ancient period. The specimens of Japanese ivory are superb and speak of the high quality workmanship. which includes the figures of Geisha girls. There are European ivories also which have been collected with a great taste from Italy, and other parts of Europe including Germany. This ivory collection may not be very old but is quite varied from various countries abroad. The artifacts of ivory have been given a significant place in the display space as a medium of art in the history of decorative arts and has an exclusive gallery for its large collection. Besides this almost all museums have a collection of ivories notable are the collection of the Prince of Wales Museum of Western India, Mumbai, the Indian Museum, Kolkata, the Govt. Museum, Chennai, the Allahabad Museum, Allahabad, the State Museum, Lucknow and the Museum and Picture Gallery, Vadodara and from every museum in India.

Incidentally the large museums all over the world are now exhibiting their Indian collections for public view especially in USA, UK & Europe. A article by Livina Melwani in Swagat, a Media Transasia publication for Air India, Sept. 2007 takes one to a guided tour of museums in the US, which have built up strong collections of Indian art spanning centuries. I did check up the web sites mentioned by her and remembered my visits to some important Museumes, US while in service.

**4. TYPES OF IVORY**

True ivory is from the elephant tusk but the large teeth of Walrus, Hippopotamus, Narwhale, Sperm Whale, Pig and Hornbill are also called Ivory. Mammoth tusks, that is fossil ivory, occurs in large amounts in Siberia and the northeastern part of the USSR. The mammoth tusks are longer and more slender than those of the African elephants. Their curvature is also quite extensive. This source of ivory came to light in the beginning of eighteenth century, according to the reports of Von wrangle and Mid Dendorf (1848-1875). Ivory was simply collected from the melting ice as well as being recovered through excavation. This was exported to china from very early times and later also to Japan. Mammoth tusks, which grew in a spiral, can be as long as measured along the curve and they sometimes weigh over 100 kg.

## (a) ELEPHANT IVORY

This category includes ivory from both Indian and African elephants, as well as ivory from mammoths and mastodon. The tusks, or upper incisors, of these animals are used. They can have a cross section of up to 20cm (8"), and be up to 2.5m (almost 3 yards) long. They are oval in cross section. They are made up of a hard, dense tissue called dentin, which is made up of 70% inorganic material, and 30% collagen. Unlike human teeth, elephant tusks do not have an enamel coating. They do have a cementum layer, and this layer is commonly known the "bark" or the "rind". Occasionally this layer is retained on a piece of worked ivory. One-third to one-half of an elephant tusk is hollow. Growth occurs as layer upon layer of calcified tissue is deposited on the interior of the tusk; you can see these concentric oval growth lines (called the Lines of Owen) in cross section. In longitudinal section, these lines appear triangular and fine and even near the hollow of the tusk (the pulp cavity), wavy and have milky areas between them as one gets closer to the outside of the tusk. Unique to elephant ivory are the Lines of Retzius. These fine intersecting lines are visible in cross section, and give an engine-turned effect (intersecting lines with a diamond shape between them). Generally, elephant ivory has a fine, even grain Ivory can easily take sawing, carving, drilling, scraping, and turning in all directions. It can be thinly cut (i.e. for piano keys), and can be more delicately carved than bone. Ivory is often painted or stained, dyed, and gilded. When cut, the pores of the ivory fill with an oily substance, which helps the ivory polish up nicely.

## (b) HIPPOPOTAMUS IVORY

This is the second most commonly used ivory, after elephant ivory. Often used for flat items, such as buttons and inlays, It comes from the lower canines and incisors of hippos. The size varies, depending on the size of the animal. The lower canine is curved, and has a triangular cross section; the incisor is straighter, and has a circular cross section. Both canine and incisor have two layers of dentin: an outer, primary dentin, and an inner, secondary dentin. The innermost layer has a marbled appearance which differs by species, and can even appear to have a greenish cast. The hard enamel of Hippo ivory must be removed with dilute mineral acid. The pulp cavities of these teeth are fairly small. Unlike elephant ivory, hippo ivory does have a thick enamel coating. Hippo ivory is denser than elephant ivory, harder to carve, and has a finer grain. There is none of the "engine turned" effect in cross section, rather, hippo ivory has concentric rings in cross section. Hippo ivory is less prone to decay than elephant ivory.

**(c) WALRUS IVORY:**

This ivory comes from the upper canines of walrus. It is over in cross section and can be over 2 feet in lenth. Cenines of Walrus have three layers. Inner Dentin layer has a high mineral content; it forms as the tusk grows, and leaves a marbled look on finished objects. Other layers are outer dentin layer and a smooth, dense cementum layer. Walrus ivory is used primarily for small objects.

**(d) SPERM WHALE IVORY:**

Thirty teeth of the sperm whale can be used for ivory. Each of these teeth, up to 8" long and 3" across, are hollow for the first half of their length. Sperm Whale ivory is easily confused with walrus ivory, as both have two distinct layers. The inner layer of sperm whale ivory, however, is much larger. As well, in a longitudinal section, sperm whale dentin has yellow "globules" included in the marbilization.

**(e) HORNBILL IVORY:**

This comes from the casque or epithema of the Helmeted Hornbill, a bird native to the East Indies. It is distinguished from the rest of its family (the Bucerotidae) by having the front of its almost vertical and slightly convex epithema made of a solid mass of horn. This "horn" or "ivory" is quite hard and closely-textured. In cross section, shows a bright yellow interior with a scarlet rim. This substance is used to make small objects such as buckles and brooches, and is highly valued by the Chinese.

### (f) VEGETABLE IVORY:

The source of vegetable ivory is the inner seed of the South American ivory palm, and is thus completely made of cellulose rather than collagen. These seeds are of the size and shape of a small hen's egg, are very hard, and are solid all the way through. Vegetable ivory is smooth, takes a good polish, easily absorbs dyes, and is relatively inexpensive. It is used for small items only, such as dice and buttons. Since about World War -II, vegetable ivory has been largely replaced by plastics.

### (g) SYNTHETIC IVORY:

Synthetic Ivory was first invented by Alexander Parkes in Birmingham, UK in 1865, by using celluloid Nitrocellulose-based plastics slightly predate celluloid: collodion, invented in 1848 and used as emulsion for photographic plates, which dried to a celluloid-like film. Celluloid went on to be used in the first flexible photographic film for still and motion pictures. Celluloid is the generic name of a class of compounds created from nitrocellulose and camphor, plus dyes and other agents like alcohol. Nitrocellulose, may be either cellulose acetate, cellulose nitrate, cellulose di-nitrate or pyroxylin. Cellulose nitrate is tough and flammable, generally obtained from wood pulp. French Ivory, Ivoride, Ivorite, Genuine French Ivory, Ivorine, etc. The word "cast ivorine" is also sarcastically applied to the synthetic ivory. Celluloid was marketed as Parkesine, Xylonite and Ivoride in 1860's by a company now known as BXL Plastic Ltd.. Both grain patterns and the engine turned effect are added. In general, the patterns of these added effects are very regular in the fakes and more irregular in the real thing. In instances of very good imitations (i.e. using celluloid), chemical tests are required to tell real ivory and the fakes apart. Ivorine and its contemporaneous commercial rivals melted at high temperatures and dissolved in acetone, while today's epoxy and polyester synthetics are easily marked with a hot needle.

## 5. TECHNIQUE OF CARVING

The first step in the creation of an ivory carving is to choose a suitable piece of raw ivory. Ivory has grain much like wood but it has the density of a soft metal. The best ivory to carve is that which is farthest away from the pulp cavity; to the outside, the ivory is the oldest and most solid and therefore the best to carve (Cutler 1985). According to Dwivedi, the Brhatsahita, composed during the Gupta period, gives instructions as to how an ivory tusk should be cut: "one should leave uncut the portion of a tusk, twice as much as its circumference at the root; and the remainder that may be cut should be used for purposes of embellishment. A little more may be cut off in the case of elephants haunting marshy places, and a little less in the case of those inhabiting mountainous tracts." (Dwivedi 1976). Because the tusk is circular, the Begram ivory carver would probably have proceeded by first sawing the circular edges lengthwise to create a rectangular piece for the plaques and bands. For sculptures in the round, this slicing would not have been necessary; such sculptures seem to have been carved each from one tusk, or perhaps half a tusk. Once the rough shape of an object had been created, the design would be outlined on the surface. In the case of the Begram objects, the design for a complete chair or footstool would have existed and each piece or element of that design would be transferred onto the required number of pieces of ivory and bone. With a chisel and a mallet, the carver would then commence the painstaking process of carving the actual design. Differently shaped chisels would be utilized for different designs. The holes needed to fasten decorative pieces of ivory were probably made by some sort of hand drill, for ivory is subject to splitting and does not lend itself to hammering. Study of nineteenth century ivory carvers has shown that when the carving has been completed, the ivory is then soaked in water, and when dry, smoothed with sandpaper (Pal 1978). The final touch is the polishing of the objects; this can be done by using the dust of the ivory (Dwivedi 1976).

Method of making of objects made of ivory and bone has to be understood well. It is also important to know as to from which part of the ivory/bone the object under consideration has been made. Whether it has been sawn tangentially or radial and whether it is a object made of a single piece or several pieces have been used in its making. Elaborate processes of carving sawing, turning, engraving, etching, grinding, polishing, staining, painting and coloration has to be studied well before actual conservation /restoration.

**(1) Carving** of ivory is more of a chipping and scrapping technique which is harder and denser than the soft wood. The ivory carver uses chisels with fairly blunt cutting edges, two and four sided scraper, burins of varied section, which are reported to be used for engraving, were made of flint in olden days, fine saws and files. Bone may be worked with the similar tools. The procedure was probably similar to that for wooden sculptures. First of all a sketch was made and probably often a model in wax though few of these have survived. Separate parts were usually put together with ivory less frequently and of box wood dowels these were glued in with animal glue.

**(2) Sawing** to make every relief's narrow rectangles were sawed out of walls of the hollow base of the tusk or out of the upper solid part of the tusk and then put together into a slab. The rectangles are relatively narrow because they are taken out of the arc of a circle. They are seldom more than 30 cm. exceptionally as much as 45 cm in length because of the curvature of the tusk. Very thinly sawn plaques (veneer) were used for inlays in furniture, boxes etc. pierced work is generally sawn out. Some examples from the Kabul Museum can be seen in the illustrations which were belonging to the period of Kaniksha from Begram.

**(3) Turning** is particularly suitable for ivories because of its homogenous dense texture and because of the ease with which it can be chipped. Ivory goblets in ancient times were made by turning. Turned objects consisting of several parts are generally screwed together - screw threads are cut into the parts to be worked with same tools. The procedure was probably similar to that of wood sculpture. First of all a sketch was made often in wax though few of these have survived. Separate parts were usually put together with ivory less frequently box wood dowels were glued in with animal glue.

**(4) Engraving and Etching:** Ornamental or figurative drawings can be engraved into ivory or bone and the incised lines may then be blacked in. Also, much as a plate is etched for printing, ivory can be covered with an etching ground the drawing then being incised in the ground and etched with citric containing dissolved silver will produce black lines.

**(5) Grinding and Polishing:** After objects made of ivory had been carved, sawn or turned the surface had to be smoothed by grinding and polishing. Wet horse-tail (Equisetum) and a slurry of the finest pumice powder were among the abrasives used for grinding; washed Tripoli powder (consisting mainly of kieselgur) whiting and Vienna lime (calcined, ground dolomite) were among the substance used for polishing. If these objects were to be painted polishing was invariably done. Some times bleaching with $H_2O_2$ was done to get the required effect.

**(6) Staining and Painting:** Ivory and bone can be stained with dye solutions. Besides the aniline dyes preferred in recent times, turmeric (yellow), cochineal, brazil wood (red), indigo (blue), logwood (violet), Oak gall with verdigris and logwood (black) and other substances have been used in the past. Japanese netsuke, e.g. were usually stained by the carver the dark or reddishbrown color of African ivory carvings is due partly to impregnation with oil and dye extracts and partly to use. The pigments and binding media used in book painting and on polychrome wood sculpture were also used to paint ivory carvings. Fine lines are incised on the surface of the material and then painted over with colored inks.

**(7) Coloration of Ivory:** Although some ivories remain creamy white for centuries, others darken or yellow. Very old ivory may resemble boxwood, chestnut, mahogany or other wood. Ancient ivory may look like slate, basalt, sandstone. alabaster and even opal or turquoise. Ivory's original color were protected from air, the piece were protected from air and ultraviolet light rays. Ivory also dries out over time and thereby loses its natural shine. Some polishing agents may restore the gloss.

CHAPTER VII

# STRUCTURE OF IVORY AND BONE

## STRUCTURE

Ivory shows annual rings like that of tree when viewed in transverse-section, as a new layer is added each year. Bone has stripes which are made of mineral crystals. Fibers and bone cells live in the small gaps between the rings. The mineral crystals give bone its strength, while the fibers help it to bend without breaking. Vegetable ivory has no rings. Walrus ivory, from the uppercanines of this vertebrate is chemically similar, but inner zone appears much more translucent, with circular opaque markings due to a higher degree of crystallinety. Hippopotamus and pig ivory are triangular in section. The hard enamel of Hippopotamus ivory must be removed with dilute mineral acid. Pig ivory is too dense to show visible grain, even under magnification. Ivory is basically an elephant tusk (upper incisors) and bone is from any large animal. Fiber of ivory is more solid than bone so ivory is smooth and bone is coarse. Unlike bone, ivory has no blood vessel system, and is, therefore, denser. Ivory contains more Magnesium phosphate and bone contains more of Calcium carbonate. They differ in their micro and macro structure. Ivory has a remarkable micro structure of very fine tubules, whose unique gyratory pattern produces the 'engine turning markings', which is missing in bone. A polished bone surface usually has small pits and what appears to be a lightly scratched surface, these are exposed 'tunnels' that permeate the bone. The crystals and fibers are produced by bone cells. Tiny channels running through the bone allow blood to reach the bone cells. Ivory is less fragile and bone is more fragile. Ivory can absorb more water than bone.

## 1. PHYSICAL STRUCTURE

To some extent ivory can be softened by very hot water or vinegar where as bone can be slightly softened by water, extensively in acid (vinegar, sour milk), which impairs its mechanical property. Ivory is mainly used for decorative purposes and bone for defense and articles of daily use. Ivory is cream colored and bone is whitish. Color of Ivory varies according to its origin. In the sunlight, Ivory bleaches. If much handled, Ivory develops a fine yellow / brown patina from the grease and other exudates of the hands. When burnt Ivory becomes gray, this feature can be used decoratively. Both of them have anisotropic (directional property) and warping tendency due to change in relative humidity and temperature. It has different mechanical characteristics along the different planes. It was reported by Kalsbeek and Richter that carbonated bone material is more prone to mechanical decay than the unheated bones due to increased brittleness on account of heat and pH. Cross sections of a mammoth tusk which is extinct now but available in fossilized forms and Walrus tusk reveal differences in internal structures. Mammoth tusks have cross-hatching and Walrus tusks have an internal core and is surrounded by rings. Ivory shows annual rings like that of tree when viewed in transverse-section, as a new layer is added each year. Where as bones have stripes. Inside a bone the rings are made of mineral crystals. It is easier to tell the difference between natural and synthetic ivories by the lack of irregular canal lines in synthetic ivory. High quality imitations can have simulated lines, but often these lines will have a repeating pattern. The safe way to detect a fake is with an ultra-violet light (UV). Natural ivory will fluoresce bright blue under UV light, and synthetics will fluoresce a dull blue. There are subtle differences between various ivories. African ivory is harder and has a translucent, yellow appearance. Asian ivory is softer and has an opaque, white appearance. Ivory is hard dense tissue (dentine) and some areas are more dense than others. The outer zone is different than the inner zones in density and structure. Bone is coarse grain and inner parts are spongy in comparison to the outer parts. There is a characteristic lacunae in bone structure and its inside is hollow. Both ivory and bone have a cellular structure which contains water vapor. Artistic visualization of the cross sectional structure and actual microscopic structures of an Elephant ivory fig. 58 and a Walrus ivory fig. 59 and bone fig. 60 can be seen as under. With the ban on elephant killing because of environmental reasons we find a large number of fake ivories coming in the market. Either bone is being sold as ivory or synthetic ivory objects which look like real ivory are being used by fakers to pass as ivory. Unfortunately the difference between the real ivory and the synthetic ivory can only be detected by chemical analysis or the SEM studies / other scientific techniques and not by simple examination by naked eye. The chemical composition of the real ivory and synthetic ivory differs as the former is inorganic and the later organic as would be discussed later.

**Microscapic view of Ivory**

**(i)** Cross Section Elephant Ivory (Plate 58) - Cross Section Walrus Ivory (Plate 59)

**(ii) Microscopic view of Bone** - Cross Section of Bone (Plate 60)

**(iii) Color** - White to yellowish. Ivory tends to yellow with age and takes on a mellow brownish yellow patina.

**(iv) Optics** - Refractive Index - I. 1.54.

**(v) Durability** - Hardness 2.5 Tough. Workable with ordinary steel cutting tools. Ivory is soft, making it a timeless favorite for carving.

**(vi) Crystal structure** - Ivory has a distinctive, "engine-turned" cellular appearance under magnification.

**(vii) Specific Gravity** - 1.7-2.0

**(viii) Conductivity** - Poor conductor of heat; Good conductor of electricity.

**Properties** -The elephant's living conditions, species, age, and sex affect the properties of the ivory. Hygroscopicity quality of ivory, bone, materials. Defines a material that has an attraction for moisture. As RH changes, it can readily take in and give off moisture which causes the material to expand and contract.

## 2. CHEMICAL STRUCTURE

Decomposition of Protein-Ossein happens by prolonged exposure to humid condition since both of them are porous in nature and hence absorb moisture. Colour is light and gets dirty easily. It is brittle due to aging. If exposed to sun light it bleaches by the photochemical action and its crystals which give a bone its strength become weak, while the fibers which help it to bend without breaking also become weak. Ivory is unique because it is classified as both organic and inorganic. The inorganic components (mineralized tissues) give ivory its strength and rigidity, while the organic components (collagen proteins) function in processes for growth and repair. Unlike bone or antler, ivory does not have blood vessels. Brittleness is there due to aging and decomposition of their essential oils. They become dark or get bleached in sunlight. They become fragile if recovered from underground alkaline surroundings of the subsoil conditions. This is also proved by scanty number in which they are found from the excavations.

**(a) Inorganic (lattice) constituents:**

* Calcium Phosphate ($Ca_2$ $PO_4$)– 50%-70%
* Magnesium Phosphate ———All the three together 0.85%
* Calcium Carbonate ———do
* Calcium Fluoride ———do
* Water—————11.85%

They differ in their ratios of hydroxyapatite ($Ca_{10}(PO_4)_6(OH)_2$) to collagen
-Bone - 1:2 :: collagen: hydroxyapatite + 5% by weight of water;
-Ivory - 1:3 :: collagen: hydroxyapatite + 10% by weight of water
-The concentration of Mg in ivory is three times higher than in bone. Ivory contains more phosphate of magnesium Newberyite, struvite and bobierrite are found as alteration products and were detected by EDX-SEM besides X-ray diffraction (XRD) and FTIR Fourier transform File. This type of analysis helps in understanding the decay process. Also ivory contains much less carbonate of lime than do bones which is a natural product.

### (b) Organic constituents

Ossein (high molecular weight protein) and Collagen matrix is 24-30% by weight. But the synthetic ivory is cellulose nitrate a synthetic product. Nearly two thirds of a bone's weight is made up by crystals of a mineral called calcium phosphate a natural product. The other third is made up by fibers of a substance called collagen. The crystals and fibers are produced by bone cells, which are scattered throughout the bone. tiny channels running through the bone allow blood to reach the bone cells.

## 3. IDENTIFICATION OF IVORY AND BONE

It is fairly easy to distinguish between varieties of complete teeth or tusks, but pieces of these are more difficult to identify. The cross-section must be carefully studied (preferably under a microscope) and compared with known samples. Particular attention must be paid to the grain of the central (pulp) cavity. Real ivory is mostly inorganic and is easily identified from the synthetic as it is cellulose base. By chemical means alone it is not possible to identify the difference between ivory and bone but microscopic examination can help as they have a definite structure. Under SEM it is still more clear. Due to shortage of genuine ivory, a lot of synthetic materials looking like ivory has got an entry in the art world.

There is urgent need to analyze the changes in the structure of ivory and bone , if any to device a proper treatment methodology which stands on scientific reasoning. DNA fingerprinting techniques may enable scientists to determine from which elephant population groups a given specimen of ivory comes (AATA abstracts 27-2172). Bone and ivory have also been dated by C14 dating by some Researchers from CCI. Studies using isotopic analysis have shown that ivory can be traced to its source area by using carbon, nitrogen and strontium isotopes. This area of study needs further research and find out data for lead, and possibly sulphur for further characterization.

Another problem which the museums world over face is the problem of identifying whether the artifact is genuine or fake. Only one case on the detection of fakes in ivory was reported in the Journal - Conservation of cultural property in India in the year 1989 by the author, while in service as the Chief Restorer of National Museum, Conservation Department, New Delhi. In this report a case study of twelve ivory bedposts, which were offered in 1988 to the National Museum for sale, were examined in the Conservation Laboratory of the museum for authentication and the author has listed the following problems in detection of fakes:

(a) Stylistic considerations which were the main flanks of detection in the earlier days showed considerable margin of errors.

(b) In the absence of adequate scientific authentication procedures, the fakes may go unnoticed.

(c) Law enforcing agencies do not have enough teeth to quickly distinguish the fakes from original and vice versa.

(d) Lack of people's awareness in the museum movement is also

responsible for fakes.
(e) Conservation scientists have not been given their due place in the museum art purchase setup as the experts need quick answers and scientific study is a job of patience.
(f) Conservation has a low priority and lack of funds is hampering the examination before acquisition.
(g) Renewed interest of museums to acquire the prized possessions also has encouraged the art dealers.
(h) Generally genuine and fake artifacts are bundled up together while offering the art objects for sale to cover up fakes.
(i) There is a shortage of artifacts in the art market and some dealers of disrepute want to be rich overnight.
(j) Lack of facilities for detection of fakes before acquisition of art objects for its collection. When I was in the Metropolitan Museum, Newyork, they never acquired an object unless proper scientific study is done and their views are heared always.

Fake Bedpost (Plate 61) induced patina and the bottom is painted with modern black paint to hide the irregular cracking (Plate 62) and genuien bedpost (Plate 63) with uniform natural patina which showed regular circular cracking (Plate 64) normal cracking.

## 4. PROPERTIES OF BONE AND IVORY

When fresh, their pores are filled with oily substance which make the carving easy and contributes for it's beautiful transparent polish in case of ivory, referred as sheen. The middle portions of the long bones are used for carving. Degreasing is done by boiling it in water or potash solution or with organic solvents followed by sun bleaching. Both have Anisotropic character, have structural defects, natural yellowing are fragile and are of breakable nature. Anisotropic (directional) property contributes to their warping due to rapid change of relative humidity and temperature. They have different mechanical characteristics along the different planes.

## 5. WATER IN IVORY AND BONE

Ivory and bone both are cellular in structure and, therefore, have a lot of vacant space in their body substance. They also contain about 11.85% water when alive but they both have to loose some of it to come to an equlibrium with a particular environment after the living body is dead. They both have directional properties and expand in high humid environment and contract in dry surroundings. Therefore, both of them are subjected to warping, cracking and splitting in the same manner as wood. It is but natural that they behave more or less like another natural material like wood. Bone and ivory are highly degradable. Because of their chemical composition, they are well preserved under certain environmental conditions and decompose quickly in others. The degree of preservation is higher in alkaline and chalky soils than water permiable soils in acid. For them the environmental conditions to be the safe limits not too humid nor low humid.

## CHAPTER VIII

# DETERIORATION OF IVORY AND BONE

## DETERIORATION

Deterioration in ivory and bone is due to the following factors:
(a) Natural factors
(b) Physical and environmental factors
(c) Chemical factors
(d) Biological factors
(e) Man-made factors
(f) Method of their making

**(a) Natural Deterioration** factors result in discoloration. New, ivory is white or pale yellow. It darkens naturally with age, becoming darker yellow or brownish. The patina which the age adds to the aesthetic value and speaks of its antiquarian value. They have an inherent nature of being fragile and easily breakable.

**(b) Physical and Environmental Decay** factors contribute to their ageing as heat, humidity and sunlight all have a part to play singly or in conjunction with each other collectively. It absorbs moisture if stored in damp conditions or cracks if allowed to dry out and loss of the moisture content. They also have directional properties due to their different coefficients of expansion and contraction in different directions. They contract in the cold and expand in the hot and humid climatic conditions. It is a brittle material being easily breakable while maintaining rigidity. In ivory and bone, embrittlement is inevitable over the course of time. Separation or break in the structure of an object, occurs due to temperature and/or RH fluctuations especially rapid fluctuations. Distortion happens due to loss of natural shape of an object (usually caused by heat or inconsistent relative humidity levels). Dryness occurs when the moisture content decreases. It has been reported that these art works get disfigured by dusty deposits of varying capacity obstructing the carving to a considerable degree and prevent them from being interpreted. It is a popular belief that some of these have been polished to get a sheen on them as these were meant for decorative purpose or have acquired the sheen naturally. It is, therefore, very necessary to find out whether the sheen is natural or intended by their makers.

**(c) Chemical Deterioration** factors decompose them in wet condition as discussed in chapter 2 above and changes happen due to their prolonged contact with water and soil underground. Breakdown of molecular bonds resulting in disintegration of the material changes happen due to their prolonged contact with water and soil underground. Salts are absorbed by them while under the soil and later travels to accumulate on the surface in the form of efflorescence hiding the minute details of the carving on their surface. Incrustation form a hard coating or crust on the surface of an object which could hide the details. Prolong contact with underground water and soil contents may result in waterlogging. In case of waterlogged finds of ivory and bone, three phases of work are strongly connected that is, conservation, restoration and reconstruction. The wet objects should not be allowed to dry quickly to deter/check the craking.

Hydrolysis of Ossein, the organic matter and its consequent disappearance results into Fossilization and its replacement by silica in the form of quartz and other salts. Action of acids disintegrates the inorganic constituents making them weak and fragile. Analytical study can also help in establishing the relationships between the burial environment, the period of immersion and the extent of digenetic change, then the understandings gained should lead to the development of a more systematic approach to the treatment especially of waterlogged ivory. Dissolution of bone happens due to biochemical and microbiological decay. This results into demineralization of the bone, damage due to the action of microbial enzymes, the microbial production and alteration of the proteins following the decomposition.

**(d) Biological Decay factors** include Fungi/fungus, microorganisms such as mold, mildew and mushrooms that subsist on the organic material they grow upon. They grow under conditions of high humidity and lack of ventilation. Black spots may also result due to dark and dirty conditions. Material being reduced to a fine loose powder. Dissolution of bone happens due to biochemical and microbiological decay. This results into demineralization of the bone, damage due to the action of microbial enzymes, the microbial production and alteration of the proteins following its decomposition.

**(e) Man Made factors of Decay** - Because of its organic nature ivory can be easily damaged if mishandled during storage, display and transportation. They can also be easily stained in contact with other materials. (e.g., rust spots from iron, green discoloration from copper, red to brown spots from rubber and leather etc.). These can break with a slight casual attitude and mishandling because of their very nature. They can also get dirty after accumulating dust and other particulate matters from the polluted environment making them aesthetically unacceptable. Modern methods of analytical procedures can identify whether the deposits are due to polluted environment or the surface has abraded/ damaged or got deteriorated due to other reasons.

**(f) Method of Making** resulting in Decay can help in knowing the reasons resulting into cracking of a handle of a dagger of ivory and bone due to rusting which increased in volume with time exerting strain on the surrounding area. A large ivory or bone object made by joining more than two pieces either by gluing or dowelling results into loosening from each other which may get separated and lost. Some of the bone images can be seen in (Plate 65) (Back) and (Plate 66) (Front) of a Female figure (Kusane) from Taxila besides (Plate 67) below from Ahichhatra are important finds of ASI now in the National Museum, New Delhi.

## CHAPTER IX

# CONSERVATION OF IVORY AND BONE

### DOCUMENTATION

On the basis of above study a complete documentation (textual, graphic and photographic both by visible and invisible radiations) a Conservator has to store the information in a Data storage and retrieval system to make the documentation systematic, meaningful, retrievable and complete in all respects. Conservation of Ivory and Bone as expected is a very difficult task especially if it has been recovered from the underground soil in excavations. This is also proved by the fact that very few artifacts of this category have been recovered from excavations. Even though their preservation in the normal surroundings in our environment and if their properties are understood well, is not that difficult to maintain them. Archaeological bone and ivory can only be cleaned, strengthened, and stabilized. Satisfactory restoration is often impossible. In archaeological sites, ossein is decomposed by hydrolysis, and the inorganic framework is disintegrated by acids. In waterlogged sites, bone and ivory can be reduced to a sponge-like material; in arid sites, they become dry, brittle, and fragmented. In some circumstances, bone and ivory can become fossilized as the ossein is replaced by silica and mineral salts Appindex-II.

## 1. CONSERVATION:

Conservators need to understand what is valued about an object in order to conserve and its relevant meaning. However, the meaning ascribed to an object is culturally specific. A conservation treatment is judged successful if it has preserved the culturally important values imposed on the object which has to be conserved for posterity. The treatment should not make any change in this to day or even tomorrow or in future. Cultures may differ from country to country but art in universal property of the humanity.

There are various steps in conservation:
(a) Eradication of biodeterioration.
(b) Cleaning of surface dirt.
(c) Removal of soluble salts.
(d) Thinning down of insoluble salts and stains.
(e) Consolidation.
(f) Treatment of waterlogged objects.
(g) Repair, joining and restoration.

### (a) Eradication of biodeterioration

Fungicidal treatment to kill the spores of microorganisms by the fumigation treatment with thymol in a closed chamber for a period of four to five days or a week or so. One can also use 5% solution of thymol in spirit for application on the affected areas to kill the fungus. Para-dichloro benzene ($C_6H_4 Cl_2$) can also be used as a repellant by spraying a solution in spirit to use would be safe.

**(b) Cleaning of surface dirt**

For cleaning there are three methods basically ie. mechanical cleaning, wet cleaning and solvent cleaning. Thus Cleaning may seem to be simple step in conservation but actually it is very complex, needs a great experience and judgment since once it has been done, it can not be undone. It is, therefore, irreversible. In the cleaning process we are required to remove or thin down the extraneous deposits or what ever has been on surface of the artifact at a particular point of time. We must consider here that the artist never intended/visualized them corroded and, therefore, were not a part of the original object when it was made. In fact we need not disturb them unless these are disturbing the aesthetic beauty, hiding of the carved details and leading further deterioration of the object in any way. Before cleaning, therefore, we must decide and ensure what needs to be dislodged and what should be allowed to remain. We must know how far to go and when to stop.

We can always begin cleaning with the gentlest method and gradually use more invasive techniques, if required. Due to ivory's sensitivity to moisture, only dry cleaning methods are safe to be used. Simple dusting with a soft hair brush to Vinyl pencil tip eraser which is a good help as they have a narrow tip and we may use a white colour vinyl tip very near to the ivory white colour for cleaning the ivory. Grated white vinyl eraser has been used successfully abroad. Gently rub the grated eraser on the ivory, using either the soft brush or your fingertip (wear white cotton gloves, so that the ivory does not absorb the oils, etc. from your hands). Later gently brush away all of the eraser flakes when the work is complete.

Cleaning by detergents (surfactants) would soften the deposits from soil, make them loose and removable later. Restrictive use of water and wiping it off with cotton swabs or buds. Washing with soap and water or alcohol (the use of alcohol will facilitate drying), followed by drying with a cotton cloth. When washing with water, it is necessary to restrict the amount of water to a bare minimum and to remain on the surface for a limited time only. Lightly scrape with wooden, plastic or metal tools. Dental tools are particularly useful for this purpose as they can reach the crevices and in dentations where dust gathered in the past and now has become dirt. Structurally weak bone and ivory must be cleaned carefully and the cleaning method used should be dictated by the specimen's condition. All this needs careful assessment forehand. Some examples of decay in Ivory and Bone are being reproduced here to show the extant of decay due to accumulations of deposits which are hiding the details of such artifacts (Plate 68) from Bhokardan and (Plate 69) Ter from India and (Plate 70) from Kabul Museum in which the parts are getting detached and lost for posterity. 'Whink' with 8% hydrofluoric acid is reported to have been used by some Restorers with success to remove rust stains followed by rinsing with careful use of water. To clean you can use ethyl alcohol or acetone with a few drops of ammonia. 15% Extran in alcohol has also been used with good results. To polish ivory you use champagne-chalk for a good shine. Flaking surface of an ivory can be fixed and held with a 2% ethyl hydroxy ethyl cellulose (EHEC) solution in industrial denatured spirit.

Lasers have found wider applications in many and varied fields spreading from science to entertainment. Conservators world over are trying to apply and practice it in the field of Art conservation as well. These include holographic documentation, nondestructive testing, laser induced ultrasonic imaging, laser-scattering surface characterization, atomic and molecular analyses, photo acoustic spectroscopy, surface modification, as well as surface cleaning of deposits, grime and insoluble salt accumulations from the surface of the ivory and bone objects by using a KrF Excimer Laser (emitting at 248 nm) within the UV radiations at lower resolutions attained by the laser which can be as low as 0.1 nm per pulse. Traditional methods of chemical cleaning are difficult to control and require extensive expertise to achieve optimum results. It is based on the removal/thinning of the unwanted grime etc. under fully controlled conditions. Surface layers of 20-300 microns thickness can be removed layer by layer. It has an additionol advantage of retaining a thin film of deposits on the surface so that the object does not look new, thus retaining its antique look since chemical cleaning is difficult to control. The initial endeavors in exploring and assessing the utility of these tools for art conservation are recounted for investigations by a large number of conservators world over. They found that especially the excimer lasers have a great potentials. Initially, laser cleaning was, by general consensus, the least possible laser application in art conservation. In the past ten years it has emerged to dominate all the other applications. Beam direction may be via manual, translational-scanner, or robotic beam positioning implemented by means of fiber optics, minors, or prisms and computer control. Substrate thermal alteration and debris re-deposition may be minimized or avoided through the incorporation of a gas jet, fluid or fluid jet, or dry-ice blast. In short, laser cleaning promises very accurate, controllable removal of unwanted accumulations from an art object. Groomstik is a natural rubber product, which is sticky and pulls the dirt off of the surface of the ivory. It is available through museum supply houses. It is used as a small piece of Groomstik which is gently rolled across the surface of the ivory and the operation is executed very delicately taking care of not to detach any loose piece or surface decorations like painting while rolling is being done.

**(c) Removal of soluble salts**

Bone or ivory from a location which is saturated with salts laden environment will invariably absorb soluble salts which will recrystallize out as the object dries. The action of salt crystallization will cause surface flaking and can, in some cases, destroy the minute details of the artifact. The soluble salts must be removed in order to make the object stable and visible to see the iconographic features. For animal fauna bones, it is usually not necessary to remove all the soluble salts. It is most efficient to rinse the bones in tap water until the chloride level in the material being treated equalizes that of the tap water or the water extract does not test for chloride. For more important artifacts made of any of these materials it advisable to remove all the soluble salts by paper pulp treatment if the object can stand it and is structurally sound or by rinsing for an appropriate length of time under tap water and then in distilled water. While faunal bone can be put directly into fresh water from seawater (there is a slight chance of cracking), the following succession of baths is recommended for important artifacts.

In order to determine the level of salts in the rinse water, it is necessary to use a conductivity meter. In most cases, one can alternatively use the silver nitrate test to detect the presence of sodium chloride. When sodium chlorides are no longer present, it is reasonable to assume that the bulk of the soluble salts has been removed. The conductivity meter measures the presence of all soluble salts and is thus a much more reliable indicator of the presence and absence of soluble salts in an aqueous solution. If the bone/ivory is structurally unsound, it can be consolidated with a 5 percent solution of Acryloid B-72 and then rinsed. The soluble salts will diffuse through the resin, though much more slowly, during the rinsing treatment.

We can dry bone/ivory in a series of alcohol baths (50% alcohol /50% water, increasing the alcohol content of the baths to 90 percent, 100 percent, and a final bath of 100 percent alcohol). For ivory, it is sometimes necessary to go through longer dehydration baths in order to ensure that the surface of the material being treated does not crack in such cases. A recommended series of dehydration baths should begin with straight water, followed by 95 percent water/5 percent ethanol (only watermiscible solvents should be used); an additional 5 percent ethanol should be then added to the bath until the artifact is in pure ethanol. To further ensure the integrity of the surface, the artifact should be placed in a second and even a third bath. The object can then be taken through two baths of acetone. In a few exceptionally critical cases, it may be advisable to take the object through at least two baths of diethyl ether. In most cases, after the object has been taken through two baths of acetone, it is reasonable to assume that all the water has been removed. The object should be then consolidated with a proper resin in order to strengthen it and to make it less susceptible to fluctuations in atmospheric humidity.

(d) **Removal of insoluble salts**

If it is necessary to remove insoluble salts or stains from bone/ ivory, some means of mechanical removal using picks or other tools is always recommended over any chemical treatment. Inevitably, some damage is done to bone and related material when stains and insoluble salts are removed by chemical means. When chemical agents are used, always make sure that the material is thoroughly wetted with alcohol before any chemical is applied. This ensures that the treating chemical remains on the surface of the artifact and is not absorbed. Structurally sound bone can be immersed in 5 - 10 percent solutions of hydrochloric acid or formic acid and we should continue to monitor the process closely. 5-10 percent oxalic acid has been used to remove iron stain from bone. For stubborn stains, 5 percent ammonium citrate used alone or 5 percent ammonium citrate followed by 5 percent oxalic acid are effective treatments. 5-10 percent hydrogen peroxide is used to remove sulfide stains. Stained bone may be placed in a hydrosulfite solution followed by dilute hydrogen peroxide to remove any remaining stain. Unsound bone should be treated with localized applications of the solution with a brush or swab. If unsound bone is submerged, the evolution of carbon dioxide from the decomposition of the $Ca\ Co_3$ will break up the specimen. Very fragile bone may require that the acid be applied locally to stubborn spots, scraped, and blotted; repeat all steps until the area is cleaned. Following stain removal, it is necessary to rinse the artifact in water to remove all residue of the treating chemical, dry in alcohol baths, and then consolidate with a resin as described below. Tools like Vibro tool must be used very carefully, needs a good control.

**(e) Consolidation**

Any resin solution must be diluted to decrease the viscosity and increase its ability to penetrate the material being treated. A 5-10 percent solution of a suitable transparent synthetic resin may be used. When large amounts of faunal bone need to be consolidated, it is experience of conservatrors that satisfactory results are achieved with water soluble PEG wax. A new treatment with a water based consolidant was tested in an attempt by some Researchers speak otherwise. To reduce the physical and chemical stresses to the objects, it was found by them that the "tried and true" organic solvent-based method was more consistently successful. When bone, ivory, or teeth are treated, slowly dehydrate them in organic solvents as described above then consolidate them with PVA (V7) or Acryloid B-72 or Acrylic resin (Primal). The use of PVA V7 is encouraged because while the molecules are smaller and are able to penetrate denser material, the resin has enough resilience to mechanically strengthen any object treated with it. For less dense material and large amounts of faunal bone, PVA with a viscosity of V 15 is recommended, since it is a stronger and general-purpose resin.

For surface consolidation, the resin has to be applied by brush. Good results can be obtained by applying a light coat of resin, allowing it to dry, and then applying a second coat. This procedure should be repeated several times in order to allow for sufficient resin to be absorbed by the material. Complete immersion of the artifact in the consolidating resin gives excellent results, while complete immersion of the artifact in the resin under a vacuum is considered to be the best method for consolidating most bone or ivory artifacts. The type of glue used to Join bone, ivory, or teeth together is to some degree dependent upon how the object was treated. If the bone or related material has been consolidated with a resin, a thick viscous mixture of the same resin should be used. PVA with a viscosity of V 25, Acryloid B-72, PVA emulsions such as Bull Dog, and in some cases, Elmer's Glue. All are also serviceable glues. Very fragile and structurally unsound ivory can be consolidated by 5% solution of acryloid B-72 however, this can be used for salt afflicted artifacts as soluble salts can diffuse through it, though slowly. Ivory statue from Bhokardan, Nagpur (Plate 71) shown earlier in (Plate 72) which was having thick incrustations and was also fragile, has been thinned down of the incrustations which were hiding the details and consolidated as can be seen from the photos of it's front and back both by me while I was Assistant Chemist (Preservation) in the laboratory of the National Museum, New Delhi and was brought by the then D.G.A. directly from Bhokardan.

The selection of a consolidant depends on the pore size of the material to be consolidated. It should not change the appearance of the artifact and it should not alter the aesthetic features. The selection of consolidant, therefore, has to be chosen very carefully with no after effects. For this purpose the important parameters to decide are viscosity, surface tension, setting time, slow or fast, changing during setting such as shrinkage and reaction with the material of the object, strength strong or weak reversibility, long term implications such as whether it will impede future analytical tests or it will loose its strength with time.

**(f) Treatment of Waterlogged objects**

The conservation of waterlogged bone and ivory is a straight forward process as is done in case of plant products such as wood. The waterlogged ivory and bone objects may be in a reduced condition to a sponge like material. The evaporation of water has to be slow using the Poly Ethylene Glycol 4000 in water or other methods of treatment like freeze drying or PEG treatment followed by freeze drying (Ellam, Diane

-1987). Complex problems seldom arise, except in cases where bone is so badly deteriorated that it can not be treated safely. In general, intensive rinsing in water to remove the soluble salts followed by complete dehydration through a graded series of water-miscible solvents, and consolidation with an appropriate resin is all that is required. Stains can be removed, but the process may damage bone if care is not taken. The only equipment required is appropriately sized containers, a selection of resins, and a variety of solvents. Some scholars find a commercial product being used abroad had good results than with the PEG treatment for waterlogged ivory and bone.

### (g) Repair, joining and restoration

Broken ivory can be fixed with PVAC-glue or epoxy resin. when the surface shows a lot of cracks, we may impregnate it with PVAC-glue dilute solution. (soluble in water). To protect the surface use of almond oil has been recommended by some workers. In the initial days we were using 10% PVA dissolved in a suitable solvent. The cracks can be filled with a filling putty which can be retouched with suitable color tone to subdue the damaged appearance. Many fragile objects of ivory and bone can be incased in a Perspex case as was done in the case of the Budhha relics from Piprawaha, photos as shown earlier are preserved in the National Museum Collection by the author when he was Head of the Laboratory. When any such damages occur, there are various methods to reverse the damages. Mildew can be cleaned and any stains removed as stated in paras above. Cracking can be restored to appeal visually and preserve the piece structurally. Specialists in "invisible" and "museum quality" restoration & conservation can replicated/ restore missing ivory elements by numerous techniques. Such work is done either from synthetic material or from real ivory, as desired by the authorities or owners. Mowilith DVD has been used for joining. Poly vinyl acetate emulsion with pH less than 6 should not be used being acidic in character. Retouching can be done if absolutely necessary and in consultation of Curators and Art Historians by following some guidelines. Retouching can be seen from six inches but it should not be visible from six feet.

## 2. REVERSIBILITY AND COMPATIBILITY

The Conservation/Restoration today is more application of science than it is an application of art. The techniques have been researched over the past decades according to the latest needs and better understanding of the materials, techniques and their decay process which has changed the thinking of the professionals regarding the attitudes and concepts in conservation. We as a matter of fact are more educated on the various aspects of the problems for which we have to find out acceptable solutions. We are, therefore, more conscious of the reversibility, compatibility, durability and aesthetics of the artifact vis-a-vis the longevity of the treatments that have been executed by way of conservation. A conservator must have today the scientific attitude but an artistic vision. It has also become a necessity since science and technology is making strides very rapidly. In conservation of art objects new materials and techniques are coming and the older techniques are becoming obsolete. It is well known today that past restoration and introduction of new materials are subject to change /deteriorate with time with the result that the changes become very conspicuous which does not go with the look of the original material of the object and hence the problem. It not only changes its look but becomes weaker after decay and needs new material /technique to restore its strength. In this context, therefore, new materials and techniques become relevant. However, well before these are actually used on the art objects, it is necessary to evaluate them from every angle so as to know about their solubility and easy removal of the decayed material from the object with out any damage to the original. This problem therefore, needs proper attention and research since reversibility and compatibility is not a theoretical aspect but has a view point which has practical implications as well. If the added material has not been subjected to any accelerated ageing tests, prior to its actual use, we would loose compatibility between the old and the new quickly because it is the belief of Conservators that the newly added material would decay quicker that the original material of the artifact even though the time is the same.

The ICOMOS charter promulgates in general the use of traditional materials or the use of any modern technique for conservation, the efficacy of which has been shown by scientific data and proved by experience. It should be borne in mind that bad restoration is no better than no restoration. If the objects are damaged for any reason which could have been avoided, no amount of conservation can bring back its original lost glory and no amount of compensation from the Insurance company can compensate the earlier glory of the object. Moreover, conservation cannot be repeated again and again because every time an artifact is subjected to conservation it is just like a surgical operation which is not without risk. Minimum Intervention, therefore, is the *mantra* supplemented by preventive conservation methods which is most important to reduce the burden on Conservators. The additional infrastructural facilities, therefore, in terms of men, material and money would always remain a big need since the collections are increasing day by day. The need of the hour, therefore, is to have a rational approach in this respect. Many Conservation experts still are not pretty sure whether reversibility is achievable or not. In my opinion we have to use the time tested materials but after evaluating and testing the facts about them after a scientific and detailed study. A material may be a good consolidant but if it is harder than ivory or bone it is not to be used since not compatible. A polymer may be well acceptable in the beginning but if it cross links after some period it may not be possible to remove it from porous material like ivory and bone.

## 3. PREVENTIVE MEASURES

When storing them wrap them individually in un buffered acid free tissue or unbleached muslin and then place them in a sealed bag of melinex or a Ziploc freezer bag. Ivory and bone artifacts should not come in close contact with each other to avoid abrasion. For cushioning ivory and bone artifacts we should never use rubber based materials since they can make them yellow. All persons who handle ivory and bone have to ensure that the hands are clean they wear cotton gloves so that they do not pass on any harmful foreign material especially from the aesthetics point of view. Curators have also to see that they are not displayed in bright lights of the sun or from electric spot light system. Always a compromise has to be ensured between the display and the conservation aspect. They should also be away from the heating system/ electric heaters and heat generating lights such as incandescent lamps. If a museum can afford fiber optics lighting system it is best from the display as well as from the conservation point of view. As regards their occasional dusting is concerned, light vacuuming or light brushing has to be resorted to ensure maximum safety. While storing the objects they should not come in contact with acidic and alkaline cushioning materials. They should be wrapped in an un buffered acid free tissue paper or unbleached cotton cloth or muslin. Later they should be kept in Ziplop freezer bags. The best protection for an ivory and bone object is to keep in a carefully controlled environment. both in terms of relative humidity (RH) and temperature. Ideal conditions are 45-55 % RH and approximately $70^{0}$ F ($21^{0}$C), with low light levels. at approximately 5 foot candles. Conditions should be kept constant: at the least. extreme conditions or rapid fluctuations should be avoided. Keeping the object in a tightly closed display case or storage drawer provides a considerable degree of buffering against sudden changes in temperature and relative humidity and is protection against dust and dirt. Dark storage also eliminates damage due to light. Bone and especially ivory objects require special care to preserve from environmental damages. Saran latex a polyvinyllidene chloride (PVDC) has been found useful by some workers (AATA -abstract 27-2169) as a moisture barrier to isolate hygroscopic bone and ivory from variation in ambient relative humidity. He has also compared it to reduce the absorption and loosing of water of these materials to that of Paraloid B-72 and polyvinyl acetate. Even though we most of time say that AC which runs round the clock is the best which is of three types namely (1) Central (2) Package (Local) and (3) Showcase or Room AC. Yet it is very difficult to maintain it round the clock for many well known reasons. The only solution, therefore, of some Alternate Technology, as described here under, seems to be of some hope. (a) Humidifiers, (b) Dehumidifiers, (c) Chemical humidifiers and de humidifiers (eg. 500 gms. of silica gel for I cubic meter space), (d) Buffering of display and storage area by keeping organic and inorganic objects together in the same space (e) using Art-Sorb (.5 to l kg. For l cubic meter space), (f) Designing of a new building to keep temp. and RH well within permissible limits by using sun breakers and shading of windows, Providing fountains and water ponds inside, (g) Use of low thermal capacity materials and (h) Use of time tested Khas-Khas to keep temperature low or keeping of plants in the display and storage areas. For this the Curators need to monitor the RH and temp round the clock using Electronic Thermo hydrographs so that they know what is to be done and when.

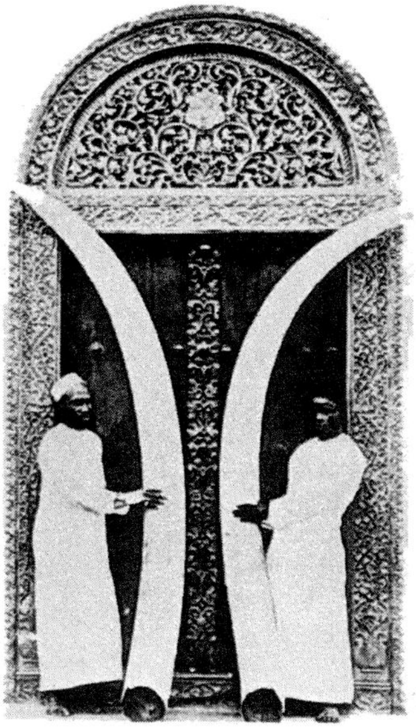

35. Tusks of African Elephant.

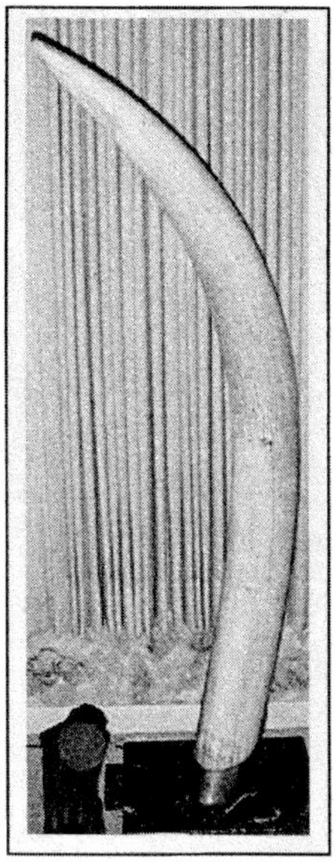

36. Tusk of an Indian Elephant

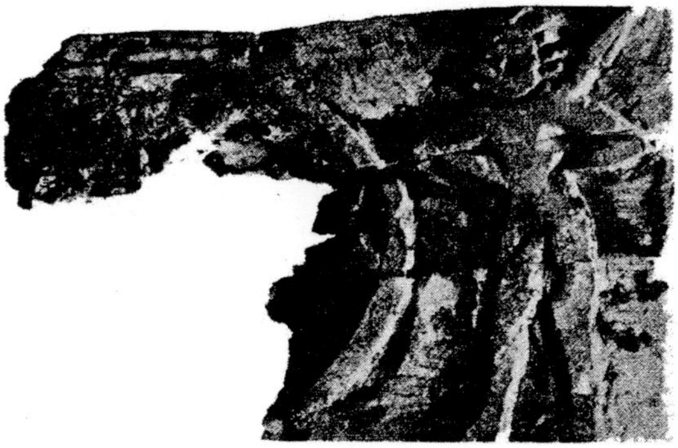

37. Plaque, Ivory, Mohenjo-daro.

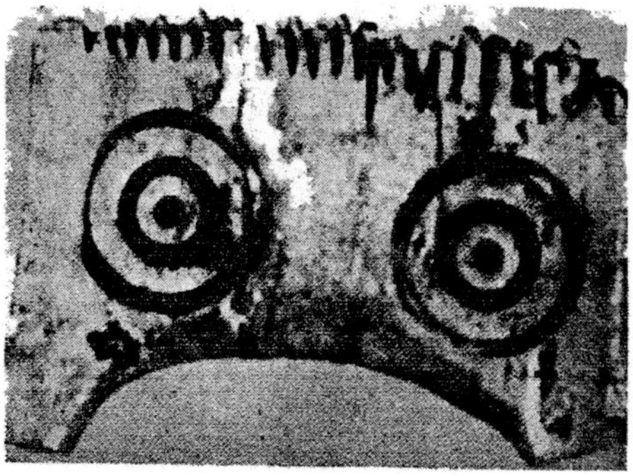

38. Comb, Ivory, Harappa.

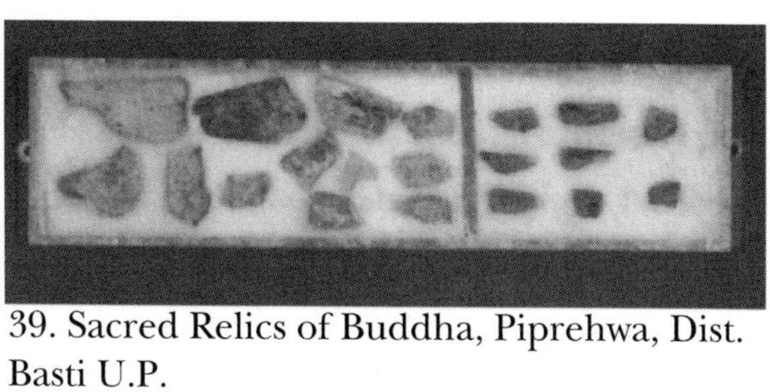

39. Sacred Relics of Buddha, Piprehwa, Dist. Basti U.P.

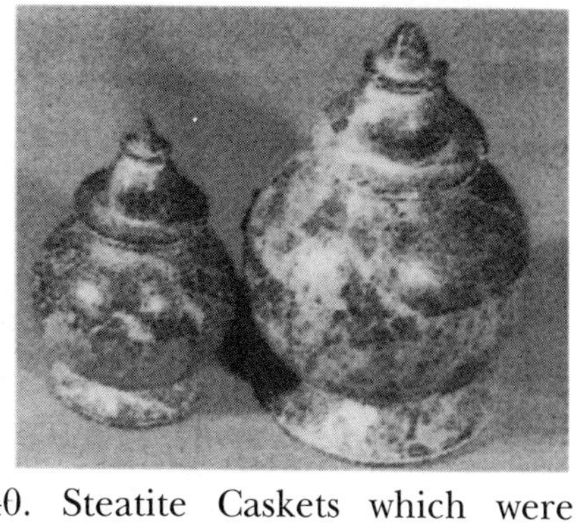

40. Steatite Caskets which were found containing the Buddha relics.

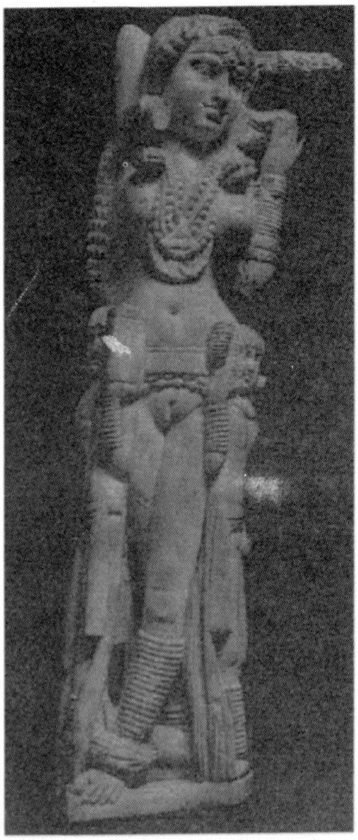

41. Ivory statue from Pompeii, Italy.

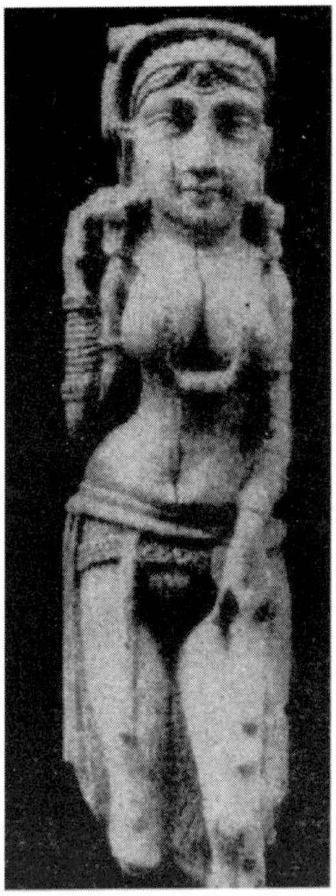

42. Ivory Statue from Ter, India.

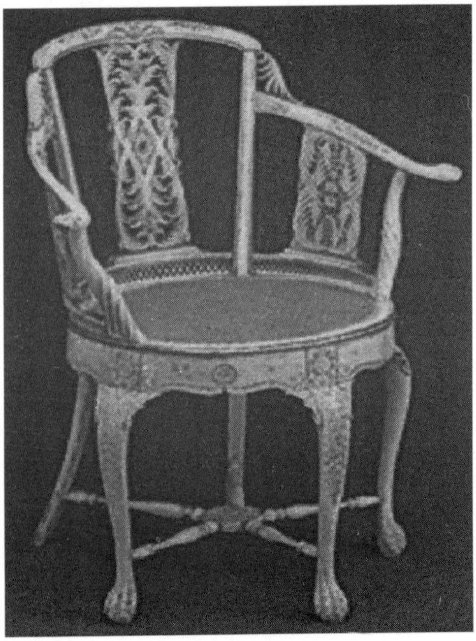

43. Carved ivory chair, Murshidabad.

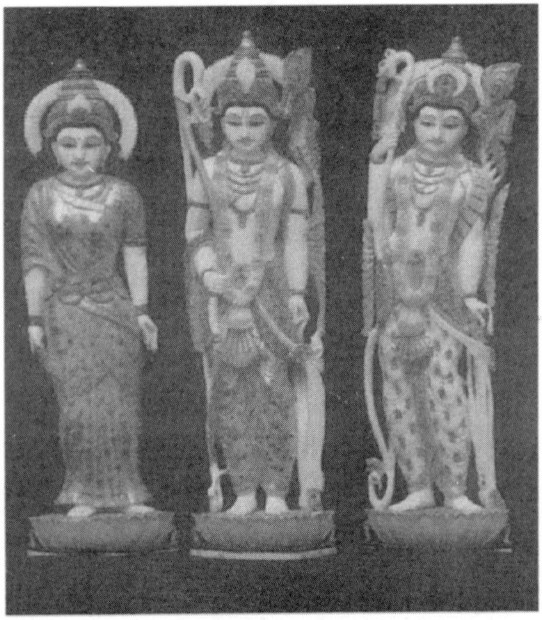

44. Ivory craft in India, images of Lord Ram, Sita and Lakshman Modem Set from Jaipur.

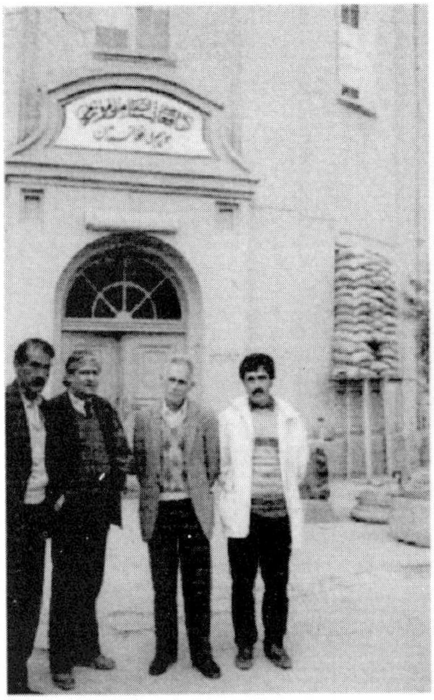

45. Afghanistans̆ National Museum, Kabul visited by the Author in 1990.

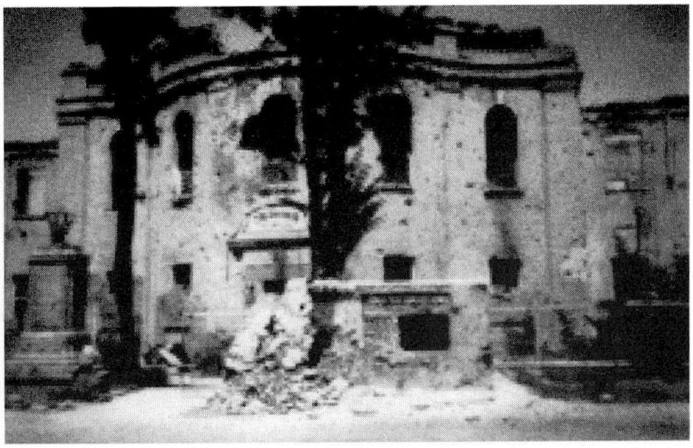

46.Same after the Taliban regime standing in Ruins

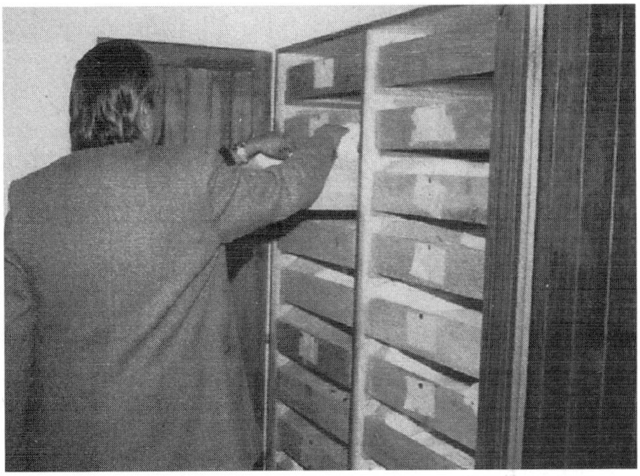

47. Author examining the ivories stored in almirahs.

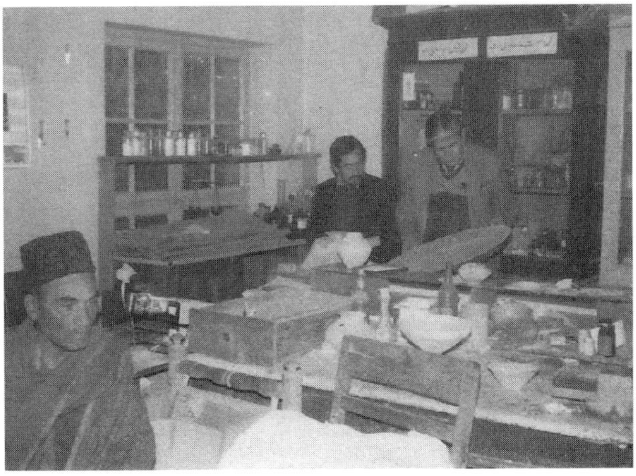

48. Author examining the artifacts in the Laboratory.

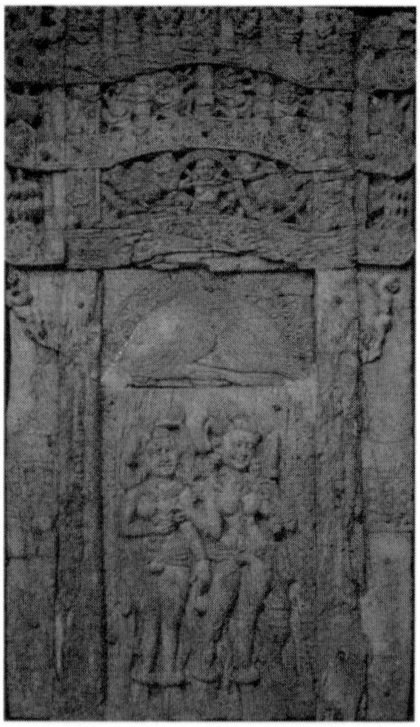

49.Begram, ivory panel, National Museum, Kabul (Guide Book).

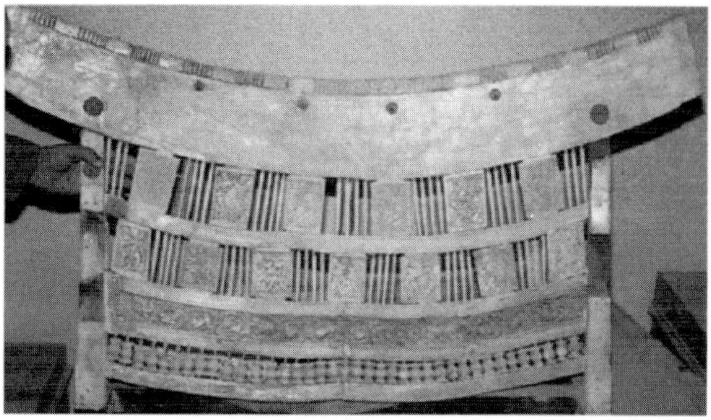

50. Begram ivory, Back of a Throne (Photo taken by the Indian Team).

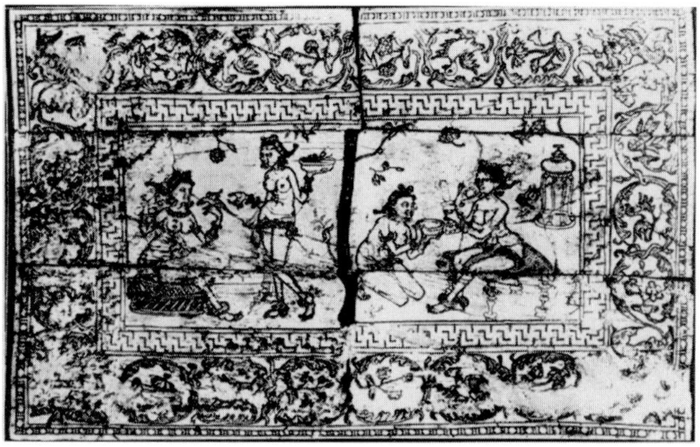

51. Segram Ivory *coffer* lid, National Museum, Kabul

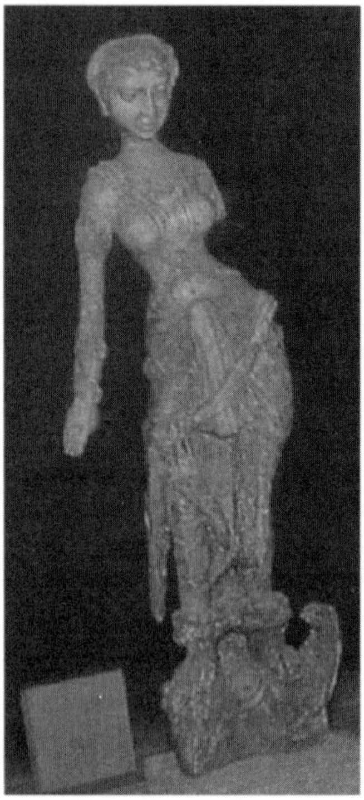

52. Begram, carved ivory Statue, National Museum, Kabul (Guide Book)

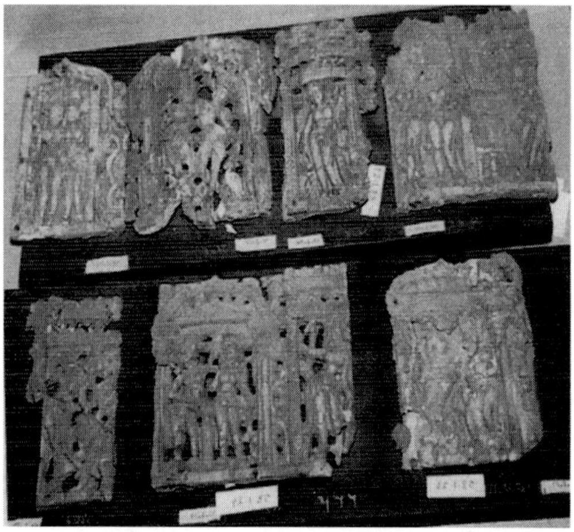

53. Begram Ivories National Museum, Kabul (Photo taken by the Indian Team).

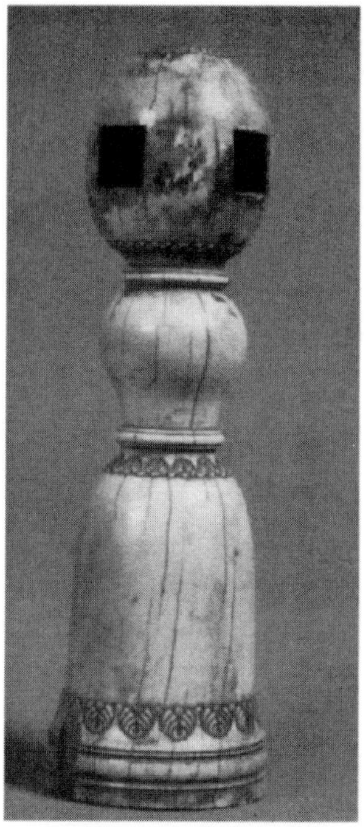

54. Plain Ivory Bedpost

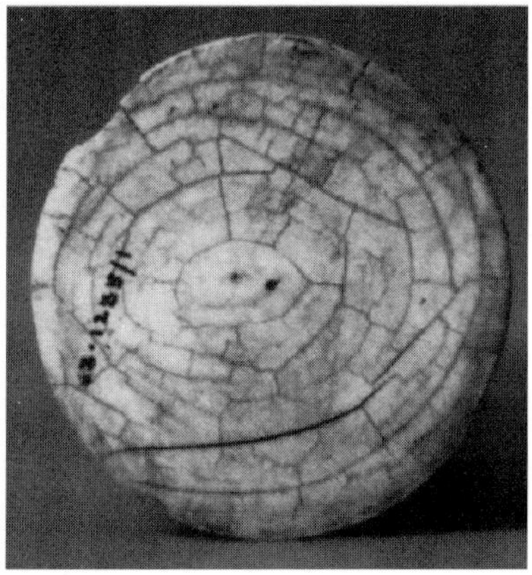

55. Bottom of the same showing regular cracking of a genuine Ivory, Orissa.

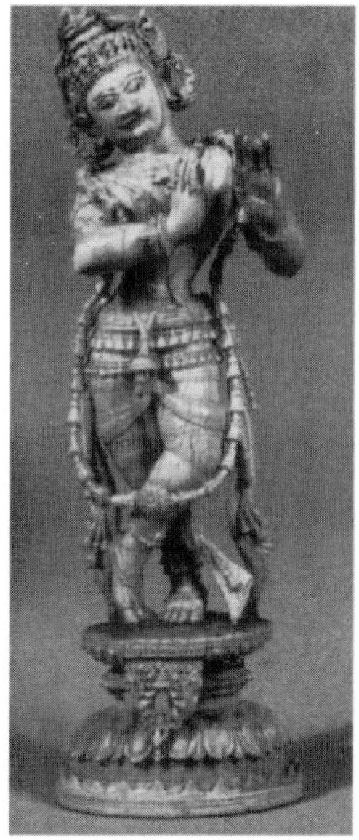

56. Lord Krishna Ivory Statue from Orissa.

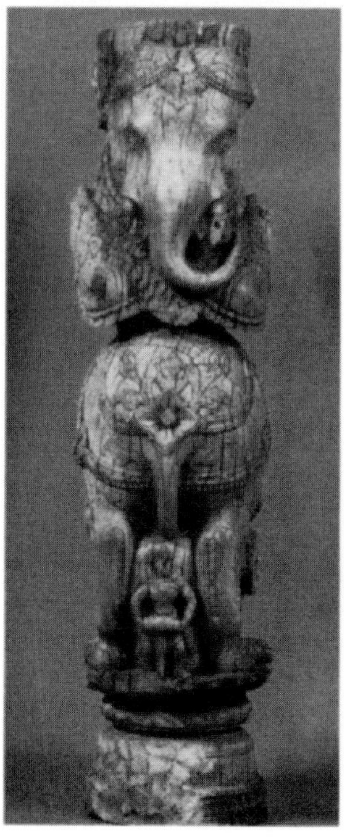

57. Ganesha Statue Ivory.

58 & 59. Microscopic View of Elephant Ivory and Walrus Ivory specimens.

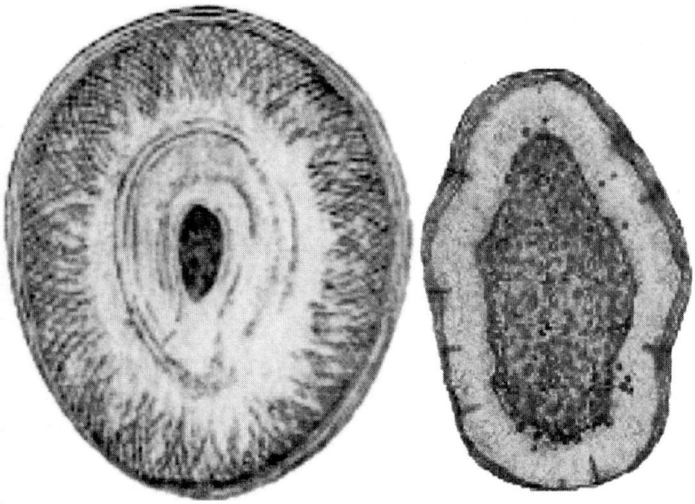

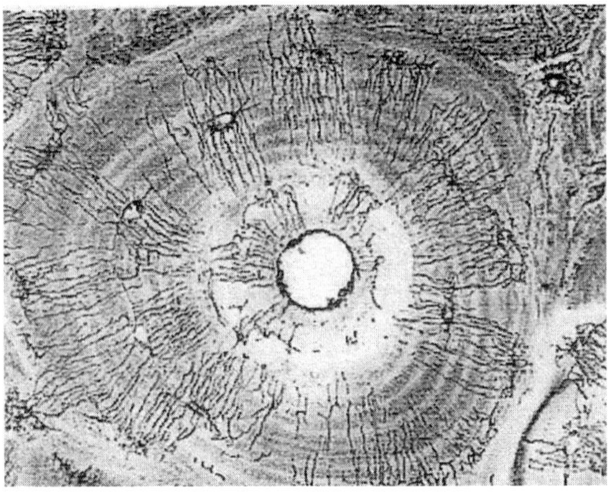

60. Nficroscopic Structure of Bone.

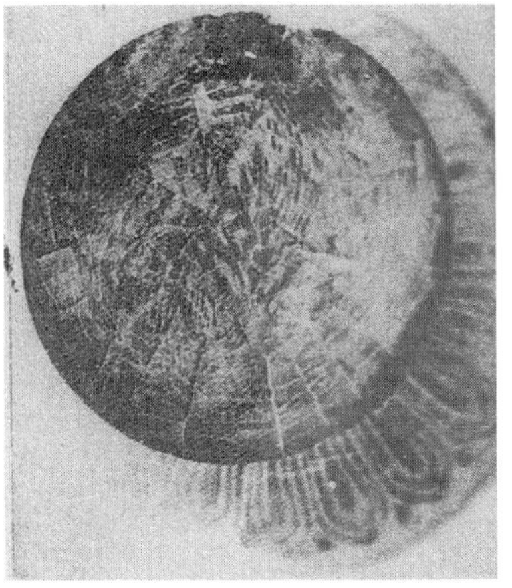

62. Bottom of the same painted to hide the artificial cracking pattern.

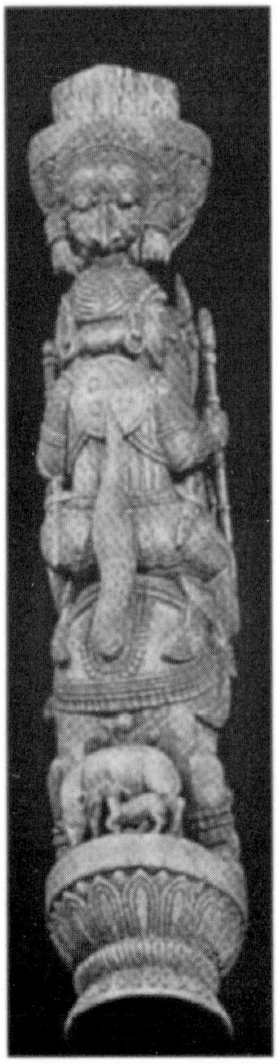

61. Fake ivory bedpost.

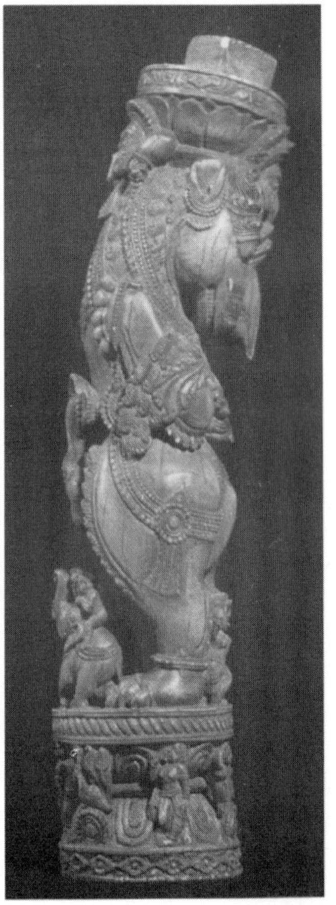

63. Genuine Ivory bedpost

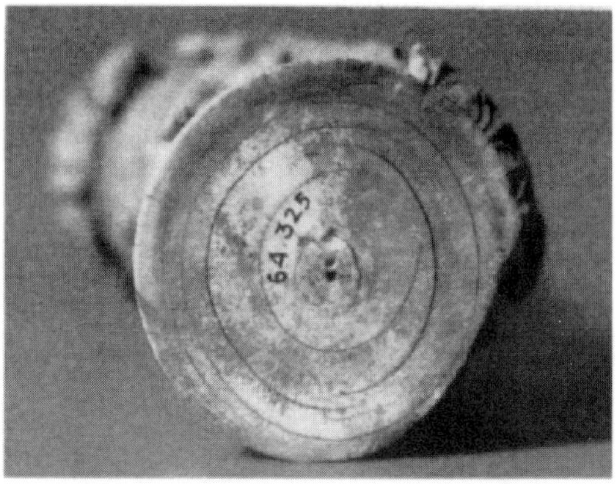


64. Bottom of the same showing normal cracking pattern.

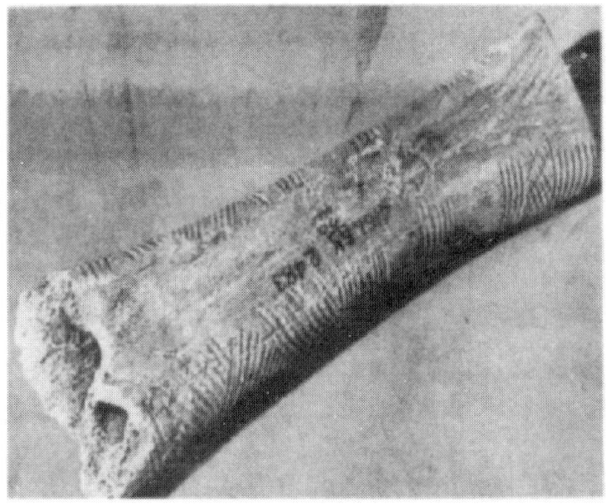

65. Back of a Bone Statue Taxsila.

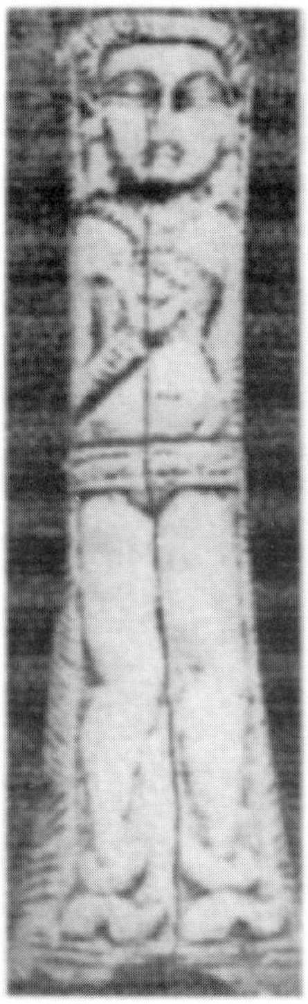

66. Front of the same bone statue, Taxsila

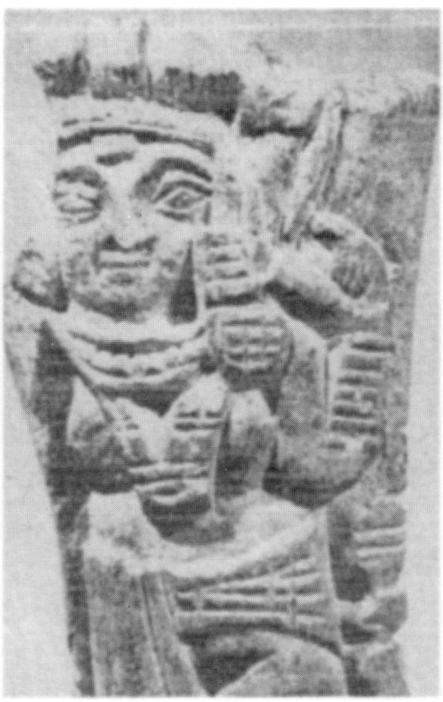

67. Bone Statue from Ahichhatra

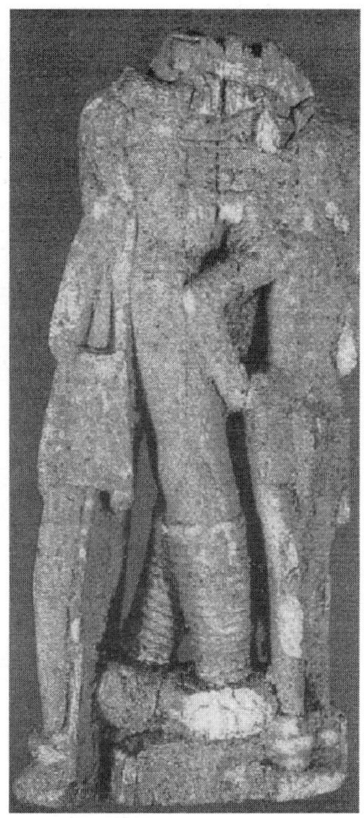

68. Lower part Back View of an Ivory Statue from Bhokardan before cleaning.

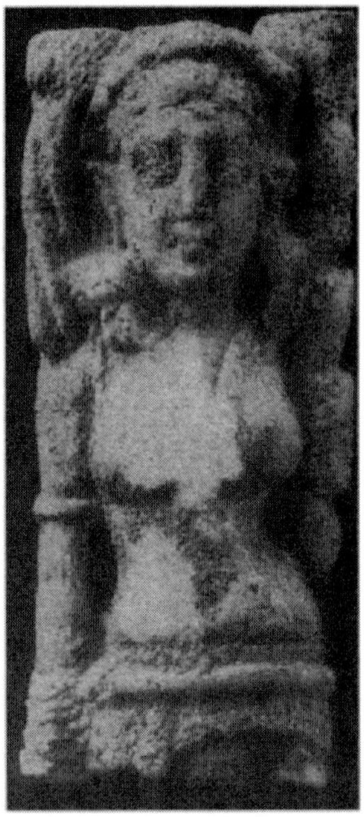

69. Uppar part of an Ivory Statue from Ter before

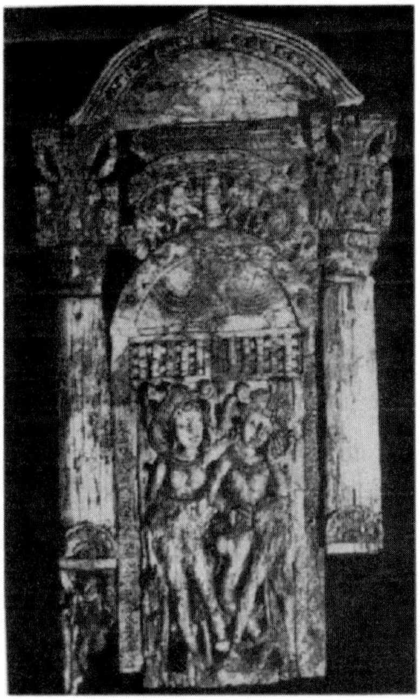

70. Ivory carving from Begram showing parts getting loose before cleaning

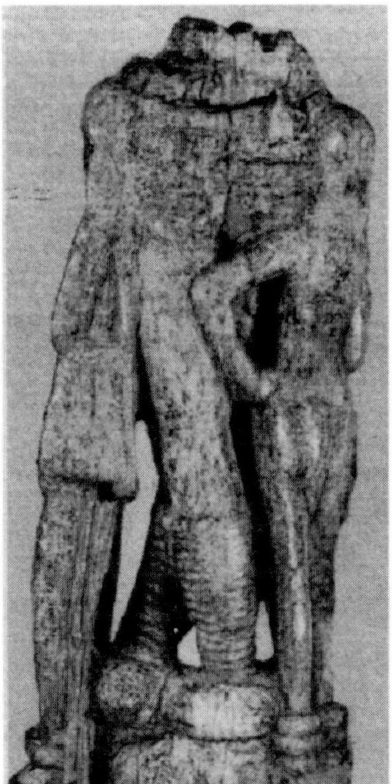

71. Ivory Statue (Back) Bhokardan after conservation.

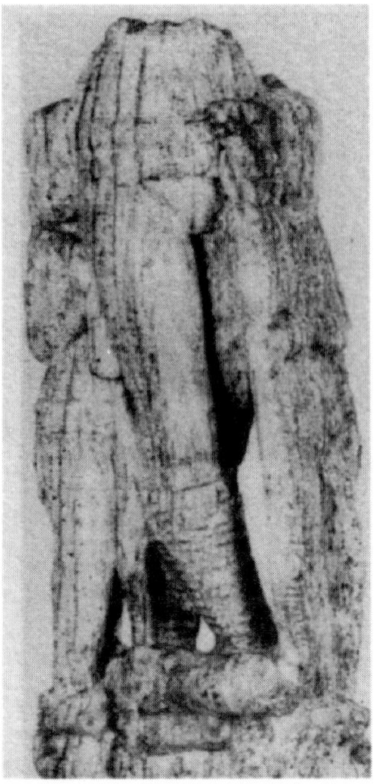

72. Ivory Statue (front) Bhokardan after conservation.

# APPENDIX - I

## TREATMENT RECORD OF TEXTILES

Date received : Examiner :
Owner : Date of return :
Owner :
Acc. No. :
Brief Description :
Provenance :
Period :
Material :
Size :
Painted/Unpainted/Dyed :
Colours visible :
Ornamentation :
Condition :
(a) Physical :
(b) Insects :
(c) Acidity :
(d) Dose it Require
(e) another support? :
(f) Stains :
(g) Fading of dyes :
(h) Are the dyes fast to washing :
Condition of Ornamentation
other :
Photography record :
(a) Nagative Nos. :
(b) Details of Photographs : Black/white & Colour
(c) Macrophotographs :
(d) Microphotographs :
(e) Slides :
Scientific study (if any) :
Treatment Proposed :

# APPENDIX - II

## TREATMENT RECORD OF MISCELLANEOUS OBJECTS
## (Other than metal, stone, textiles, wood, paper and painting)

Examiner :
Date of return :

Date received :
Owner :
Acc. No. :
Brief Description :
Period :
Provenance :
Material of the object :
Shape and Size :
Condition :
(a) Physical :
(b) Insects :
(c) Salts :
(d) Others :
Photography record :
(a) Nagative Nos. :
(b) Details of Photographs :
(c) X-ray :
(d) Marco & Micro photographs:
(e) Slides :
Ane other observations :
Scientific Analysis (if any) :
Treatment Proposed :

# BIBLIOGRAPHY


| | |
|---|---|
| Jaykar, Pupul, | 'Indian Textiles Through the ages: Treasures of Indian Textiles', Marg Publications , Mumbai (1980). |
| Gopal, Lallanji , | 'The Textile Industry in Early Medieval India (c.A.D. 700-1200), The Journal of the Asiatic Society of Bombay, Vol.39/40 (1964-65), pp.95-103. |
| | 'Memoir of the Archaeological Survey of India', No.73, pp. 55-56. |
| Agrawala, V.S., | 'Kadambari'. |
| Motichandra, | 'Prachina Bharatiya Vesa-bhusa'. |
| Cordier, | 'Yule's Travels of Macro Polo,' Vol.II, pp.391. |
| | 'Rig Veda,'Vol.55.6. |
| Elliot and Dowson, | 'History of India as told by its own Historians' Vol. I. |
| Naqvi, Hamida Khatoon, | 'Colour making and dyeing of cotton Textiles in medieval Hindustan, Indian Journal of History of Sciences, Vol.XV, No.1 (1980), pp.58-70. |
| Geijer, A., | 'The Conservation of Textile Objects' Museum, Vol. XIV No.3 (1961), pp.161-164. |
| Geijer, Agnes, | 'Preservation of Textile Objects' Studies in Conservation,Vol.6, No.4, Rome conference (1961), pp.144-145. |
| Bengtsson, S., | 'Preservation of the Wasa Sails. In Conservation |

in Archaeology and the Appled Arts', (1975) pp. 33-35. IIC, London

Annis and Reagan, 'Evaluation of Selected Bleaching Treatments Suitable for Historic white cotton', Studies in Conservation, Vol.24 (1979), pp.171-178.

Erling, J.A., 'The Treatment of Waterlogged Textiles from the Excavation of the Machault', Paper presented to the Annual SHA/CUA Conference, Ottawa, Canada (1977).

Landi, S. & R.M. Hall 'The Discovery and Conservation of an Ancient Egyptian Linen Tunic',. Studies in Conservation ,24(1979),pp.141-152.

Marko, K.& 'The Conservation of an Eighth-Century A.D. Sleeveless

M. Dobbie, Coptic Tunic'. Studies in Conservation, Vol.27 (1982), pp.154-160.

Smith, C. Wayne, 'Archaeological Conservation Using Polymers', Texas A&M University Anthropology Series, Number Six, Texas A&M University Press, College Station, Texas (2003).

Tilbrook, D. R., & C. Pearson, 'The Conservation of Canvas and Rope Recovered from the Sea', In Pacific Northwest Wet Wood Conference Proceedings, edited by G. H. Grosso, pp. 61-66. Pacific Northwest Wet Wood Conference, Neah Bay, Washington (1976).

Leene, Jentina , 'Textile Conservation', Butterworths for The International Institute for Conservation, London.

Bellinger, Louisa, 'Basic Habits of Textile Fibers' Studies in Conservation, Vol.6, No.4, Rome conference (1961), pp.145-146.

Beecher, E.R., 'Reinforcing Weakened Textiles With Synthetic–Fibre Net', Studies in Conservation, Vol.6, No.4, Rome conference (1961), pp.146-147.

Finch, Karen, 'Conservation of Dress worn by Mary Birch, 4 Years old in 1812', Studies In Conservation, Vol.8, No.3 (1963), pp.106-107.

Lehmann, Detlef, 'Conservation of Textiles At The West Berlin State Museums' Studies in Conservation, Vol. 9, No.1 (1964), pp. 9-22.

Rice, James W, 'A Drycleaning Technique For Textile Conservation' Studies in Conservation, Vol. 9, No.3 (1964), pp.83-90.

Withers, M.C., Markel, Gertrude & Cavallo, A.S., 'A Dry Method of Cleaning Metallic Yarns and Ornaments in Textiles,' Studies in Conservation, Vol.9 No.3 (1964), pp. 91-106.

Rice, James W, 'An Heirloom Patchwork Quilt and it's Conservation Problems' Studies in conservation, Vol.11, No.1 (1966), pp.8-30.

Padfield,T. & Landi,S. 'The Light Fastness of the Natural Dyes', Studies in Conservation Vol. XI (1966), pp.181-195.

Crews, P.C., 'The Fading rates of some natural dyes', Studies in Conservation, Vol.XXXII (1987), pp.65-72.

Bhatt, B.N., 'Catalytic fading of in textiles' Textile Dyer and Printer (1988), pp.17-18.

Indictor, N., Koestler, R.J., Wypyski, M. & Wardwell, A.E., 'Metal threads of Proteinaceous subtstrates examined by Scanning electron microscopy energy dispersive X-rays spectrometry', Studies in Conservation, Vol.34, No.4 (1989), pp.171-182.

Skals, Irene, 'Metal Threads with Animal-Hair Core', Vol.36, No.4 (1991), pp.240-242.

Ford, Bruce L., 'Monitoring colour change in Textiles on Display' Studies in Conservation,Vol.37, No.1 (1992), pp. 1-11.

Brimblecombe, Peter, Shooter, David & Kaur, Ajit, 'Wool and Reduced Sulphur Gases in Museum Air', Studies in Conservation, Vol.37, No.1 (1992), pp.53-60.

Halvorson, B.G. & 'Effect of light on the Properties of Silk fabrics

Kerr, Nancy, Coated With Parylene-C', Studies in Conservation, Vol.39, No. 1, (1994), pp. 45-56.

Rivers, Shyane, 'Conservation of Japanese Laacquer in Westren collections: Conserving meaning and substance', Priprints 14th Triennal Meeting The Hague (12th-16 september 2005), Vol.II, pp.1083-1086.

Oddy, W.A., 'An unsuspected danger in display', Museums Journal 73 (1973), pp. 27-28.

Kharbade, B.V. & Agrawal, O.P., 'Analysis of Natural dyes in Indian Textiles' Studies in Conservation,Vol.33, No.1 (1988), pp.1-8.

Becker, M.A., Manghoshi, Yoshiko, Sakai, Tetsuya & Tuross, N.C., 'Chemical and Physical Properties of Old Silk Fabrics' Studies in Conservation, Vol.42, No.1 (1997), pp.1-10.

Kohara, Natsuko, Sasa Yoshiko, Uda, M., & Sakurai, Kiyohiko 'A Note on the characerization of Metal Threads in Historic Textiles Handed down by the Ainu People', Studies in Conservation, Vol.43, No.2 (1998), pp.109-113.

Peacock, Elizabeth, E., 'A note on the Effect of Multiple Freeze-Thaw Treatment on Natural Fibre Fabrics', Studies in Conservation, Vol.44, No.1 (1999), pp.12-18.

Daniels, Vincent, 'Factors affecting the deterioration of the cellulosic fibres in black-dyed New Zealand flax', Studies in Conservation, Vol. 44, No.2 (1999), pp.73-85.

Nord, A.G. & Tronner, Kate, 'A Note on the Analysis of Gilded Metal Embroidery Threads'Studies in Conservation, Vol.45, No.4 (2000), pp. 274-279.

Tronner, Kate, Nord, A.G., Sjostedt, Jaennie & Hydman, Hubert, 'Extremely Thin Gold Layers on Gilded Silver Threads' Studies in Conservation, Vol.47, No.2 (2002), pp.109-116.

Garside, Paul & Wyeth, Paul, 'Identification of Cellulosic Fibers by FTIR Spectroscopy', Studies in Conservation, Vol. 48, No.4, (2003), pp. 269-275.

Rowe, Sophie, 'The Effect of Insect Fumigation by anoxia On Textiles Dyed with Prussian Blue' Studies in Conservation, Vol.49, No. 4 (2004), pp. 259-270.

Ragauskiene, Daina, Niaura, Gediminas, Matulionis, Eimutis & Makuska, Rieardas, 'Long-Term and Accelerated Ageing of an Acrylic Adhesive Used as a Support for Museum Textiles' Studies in Conservation, Vol.51, No.1 (2006), pp. 57-68.

Bergstrand, Margareta & Hedhammar, Erika, 'European Metal Threads in Swedish Churches 1600-1751–Construction and Conservation', Studies in Conservation, Vol.51, No.1 (2006), pp.11-28.

Kite, Marion & Cogram, Albertina, 'Re-evaluation and Retreatment, The Reconservation and Remounting of an English Court Mantua Studies in Conservation, Vol.51, No.2 (2006), pp.111-122.

Timar-Balazsy, Agenes, 'Wet cleaning of historic textiles: surfactants and other wash bath additives', Reviews in Conservation, IIC, No.1 (2000), pp.46-64.

Gill, Kathryn, 'The development of upholstery conservation as a practice of investigation, interpretation and preservation', Reviews in Conservation, IIC, No.5 (2004), pp.3-22.

Schweppe, H., 'Identification of Dyes in Old Textiles,' J. American Institute for Conservation, Vol. XIX, No.1 (1980), pp.14-23.

Nair, S.M., 'Dermestid beetles-A threat to museum collections in India' Conservation of Cultural Property in India (Prof. G.N. Pant Commemoration Volume), Ed. A.S. Bisht, I.K. Bhatnagar & S.P. Singh, (2000), pp.157-159.

Agarwal,O.P. & Bisht,A.S., 'Mounting of weakened textiles' Conservation of Cultural Property in India (Prof. G.N. Pant Commemoration Volume), Ed. A.S. Bisht, I.K. Bhatnagar & S.P. Singh (2000), pp.210-213.

Hot chand, 'Conservation Of A Persian Carpet' Conservation of Cultural Property in India, Vol. VI (1973), pp. 86-87.

Prasad, Lalan Kumar, 'Cleaning of simple or Brocaded Silk and Woolen Fabrics with the help of Ritha and Shikakai' Conservation of Cultural Property in India, Vol. XIV-XV(1981-82), pp.35-40.

Anand ,O.P., 'Neem as a Medicinal Plant', Science Reporter, Vol.XIII, No.2 (1976)

Kharbade, B.V. & Agarwal, O.P., 'Identification of Natural Dyestuffs in Old Textiles: Application of TLCIR Techniques' Conservation of Cultural Property In India, Vol. XIV-XV, (1981-1982), pp.68-73.

Uniyal,C.P., 'Conservation of A Fragile textile (A Kurtani Having Zari Work) With A New Approach In Its Reinforcement', Salar jung Museum Bi- Annual Research Journal, Vol. XI-XII (1978-79), pp.1-5.

Bisht, A.S. & Naithani, H.K., 'Identification of Central Asian Textiles of LAU-LAN Area'Conservation of Cultural Property in India, Vol. XIV- XV, (1981-1982), pp.74-85.

Krishna , Riboud, 'Essential Problems Concerning Central Asian Silks', Journal of Indian Museums, Museums Association Of India, Vol. XXV-XXVI (1969-1970), pp.56-63.

Jeyaraj, V. 'A Technical study of Selected Kalamkari Textile of Govt. Museum, Madras', Conservation of Cultural Property in India, Vol. XIV-XV, (1981-1982), pp. 86-89.

Bisht, A.S., 'Strengthening of Fragile Textiles-A View point', Conservation of Cultural Property in India, Vol. XIV-XV (1981-82), pp. 90-94.

Kalyanraman, A.R., 'X-ray Orientation and Dating of Archaeological Fiber Artifacts'Conservation of cultural Property in India, Vol. XIV-XV (1981-82), pp. 62-67.

Hotchand, 'Conservation of Textile Exhibits 'Conservation of Cultural Property in India, Vol. XIV-XV (1981-82), pp. 98-99.

Nair, S.M., 'Insect Pests of Textile Material in Museums', Conservation of Cultural Property in India, Vol.XIV-XV, (1981-82), pp.100-105.

Mathur, Dinesh K., 'Deterioration of Textiles and their Conservation', Conservation of Cultural Property in India, Vol. XIV-XV, (1981-82), pp.106-110.

Gupta, C.B., 'Conservation Treatment of Pichwais' Conservation of Cultural Property in India,Vol. XIV-XV (1981-82), pp.111-114.

Rao, J. Venkata & Subramaniam, V., 'Storage and Display of Textile Material in Museum', Conservation of Cultural Property in India, Vol. XIV-XV (1981-82), pp.115-124.

Naithani, H.K., Bisht, A.S., 'Technique Employed to prepare the Cross Section to Study the Brittle and Fragile Fibers', Conservation of Cultural Property in India, Vol. XVI-XVII (1983-84), pp.67-70.

Indictor, N. & Bisht, A.S., 'The Examination of Metal from Historic Indian Textiles in the National Museum, New Delhi, using Scanning Electron Microscope-Energy dispersive X- Ray Spectrometry', Conservation of Cultural Property in India, Vol. XXII (1989), pp.133-139.

Bandyopadhyay, Manasi, 'Damage Caused by Larvae of Anthrenus flavipes lec. (Vorex Waterh) on Woolen Fabrics,' Conservation of Cultural Property in India, Vol. XXII(1989), pp. 104-107.

Naithani, H.K. & Kharbade, B.V. , 'An Overview on the Consideration of Cleaning of Historic Textile' Conservation of Cultural Property in India, Vol. XVIII-XX (1985-87), pp.35-40.

Bisht, A.S. & Naithani, H.K., 'Conservation Oriented Technical Study of the Mechanism of Deterioration of a Jamewar Shawl', Conservation of Cultural Property in India, Vol. XVIII- XX (1985-87), pp. 27-30.

Uniyal, C.P. & Humane, K.A., 'Technical Study and Conservation of Kalamkari Paintings –A case study', Conservation of Cultural Property in India,Vol. XIX (1996), pp.253-258.

Agarwal, O.P., 'Problems in Conservation of Textiles', Bulletin of Museums & Archaeology in U.P., No.7, (1977), pp.1-13.

Agrawal, O.P., 'Conservation Of Textiles', Treasures of Indian Textiles, Marg Publication, 1980, Calico Museum , Ahmedabad pp.135-142.

Jain, Ritu, 'Preservation of Textiles in Museums', Journal of Indian Museums (Golden Jubilee volume),Vol. XXXXIX-L (1993-94), Museums Association of India, New Delhi, pp.211-219

Agrawal, Usha, 'Conservation Practices of Textiles in India', Recent Trends in Conservation of Art Heritage (Dr. O.P. Agrawal Festschrift) ed. Dr. Shashi Dhawan, Agam Kala Prakashan, Delhi (1995), pp.37-54.

Plenderleith, H.J., 'Conservation of Antiquities and Works of Art' Oxford University Press, Second Edition (1971).

Landi, Sheila, 'The Textile Conservator's Manual - Second Edition', Butterworth-Heinemann Oxford (2002).

Balazsy Timar, Agnes & Eastop, Dinah, 'Chemical Principles of Textile Conservation', Butterworth Heinemann (2002).

Landi, Sheila, 'Textile Conservation in the V &A Museum,' Preprints of the 4th Triennial of the ICOM Committee on Conservation,Venice, 1975, Vol.2. pp.75/10/1-9.?

Vetter, A. & Bauer, W.P., 'Pest control in Ethnographic Museums by means of.Fumigation'Preprints of the 5th Triennial

Meeting of the ICOM Committee for Conservation, Zagreb, 1978.

Smith, A.W. & Lamb, M.H., 'The Prevention of redeposition in the cleaning of ancient textiles', Preprints of the 6th Triennial Meeting of the ICOM Committee on Conservation, Ottawa, 1981, pp. 81/9/4-1.

Cater, J.W., 'Iron stains on Textiles a study to determine their nature and to evaluate current treatments,' Preprints of the 7th Triennial Meeting of the ICOM Committee on Conservation, Copenhagen, ICOM with the J. Paul Getty Trust, 1984, pp. 11-14.

Eastaugh, N., 'Some experiments comparing the performance of detergent formulations based an an ionic and nonionic surfactants under conditions relating to conservation use', Preprints of the 8th Triennial Meeting of the ICOM Committee for Conservation, Sydney, The Getty Conservation Institute Marinadel Rey, 1987, pp. 357-364.

Goilikov, V.P. & Ustinov, S.V., 'Complex experimental investigation of the effect of cleaning compositions on the fibers and dyes of Museum textiles', Preprints of 8th Triennial Meeting of ICOM Committee for Conservation, Sydney, The Getty Conservation Institute, 1987, pp. 373-377.

Grattan, D.W., 'Parylene at the Canadian Conservation Institute: an initial survey of some applications' in ICOM Committee for Conservation, 9th Triennial Meeting, Dresden (1990), pp.1-10.

Shashoua, V., 'Investigation into the effects of cleaning natural, woven textiles by aqueous immersion', Preprints of the 9th Triennial Meeting of the ICOM Committee for Conservation, Dresden, ICOM, 1990, pp. 313-318.

Shashoua, Y., 'Investigation into the effects of cleaning old, dyed, naturally soiled textiles by Aqueous immersion', Preprints of the 10th Triennial Meeting of the ICOM Committee for Conservation, Washington DC, 1993, pp. 714-720.

Timar- Balazsy, A, Matefy,G. & Csanyi,S., 'Effects of stains and stain removal methods on historical textiles', Preprints of the 10th Triennial Meeting of the ICOM Committee for Conservation, Washington DC, James & James London, 1993, pp.330-335.

Boring, M. & Ewer, P., 'Report on test performed to determine the optimal concentration of The surfactant Orvus WA paste for cotton', Preprints of the 10th Triennial Meeting of the ICOM Committee for Conservation, Washington DC, 1993, pp. 289-293.

Ballard, M.W., 'The removal of cross linked synthetic latex from carpets: preliminary results' Postprints of the 10th Triennial Meeting of the ICOM Committee on Conservation, Washington DC, James & James, London, 1993, pp.331-338

Reponen, T.H., 'The effect of conservation wet cleaning on standard soiled wool fabric: some experimental work', Preprints of the 10th Triennial Meeting of the ICOM Committee for conservation, pp.321-326.

Carrwright, H. & Colombini, A., 'Detergent monitoring during washing process at the textile Conservation Studios, Hampton Court Palace', Preprints of the 10th Triennial Meeting of the ICOM Committee for Conservation, Washington DC, 1993, pp. 293-298.

Rhee, H. & Ballard, M., 'Residues of surfactant on silk', Preprints of the 10th Triennial Meeting of the ICOM Committee for Conservation, Washington DC, 1993, pp. 327-329.

Pataki A., 'Restoration of a 16th cent. child's coat('mente') belonging to the Esterhazy collection', Preprints of the 10th Triennial Meeting of the ICOM Committee on the Conservation, Washington DC, 1993, pp. 314-320.

Keyserlingk, M., 'Conservation and co-operation: treatment of the table-woven Gondar hanging at the Canadian Conservation Institute', Preprints of the 10th Triennial Meeting of the ICOM Committee for conservation, Washington, DC, 1993, pp. 699-703.

Eastop, D. & Brooks, M., 'To clean or not to clean?' Preprints of the 11th Triennial Meeting of ICOM Committee, for Conservation, Edinburgh, James & James, London, 1996, pp. 687-691.

Johansen, K., 'Perfumed garments, their preservation and presentation of the good smell of old clothes', Preprints of the 12th Triennial Meeting of the ICOM Committee of Conservation, Lyon, James & James, London, 1999, pp.637-642.

Bruselius -Scharff, A., 'Synthetic Dyestuff for textiles and their fastness to washing', Preprints of the 12th Triennial Meeting of the ICOM committee for Conservation Lyon, James & James, London, 1999, pp.654-660.

Karsten, Irene F. & Down, Jane, 'The effect of adhesive concentration, reactivation time, and pressure on peel strength of heat and solvent-reactivated Lascaux 360/498 HV bonds to silk', Preprints14th Triennial Meeting of the ICOM Committee for conservation, Hague (12-16, September 2005), Vol. II, pp. 927-935.

Rice, J. W., 'Principles of fragile textile cleaning', Textile Conservation, Butterworth, London, 1972, pp. 32-72.

Kuhn, Hermann , 'Conservation of Works of Art and Antiquities, Butterworth-Heinemann, London.

Oddy, W.A., 'An Unsuspected danger in Display', Museums Journal, Vol.73, pp.27-28.

Thomson, G. 'The Museum Environment', Butterworths, London (1978).

Harvey, Janet, 'Traditional Textiles of Central Asia', Thames and Hudson Ltd. London (1996). 'Ancient Rome and India,' ed. Rosa Maria Cimino and published by the Italian Embassy Culture in Delhi, printed by Munshiram Manoharlal Publishers Pvt. Ltd, New Delhi.

Moti Chandra, 'Costumes, Textiles, Cosmetics & Coiffure in Ancient and Mediaeval India', Oriental Publishers, Delhi (1973). pp.29.

Jayakar, Pupul, 'Naksha Bandhas of Benaras', Journal of Indian Textiles History, No.7, pp. 22.

Lal, Krishna, 'Technique of Bandhana or Tie-Dyed Fabrics', Journal of Indian Museums Vol. XXV-XXVI (1969-70), pp. 93-95.

Bisht, A.S., 'Prevention and Eradication of Biodeterioration in Museums, A Study of Problems and Future Prospects', Journal of Indian Museums, Vol. XLIII (1987), Museums Association of India, pp.163-168.

Bisht, A.S. 'New Approach in Conservation of Textiles: Curative and Preventive', National Museum Bulletin ed. R.R.S. Chauhan, National Museum, New Delhi Nos.7&8 (1993), pp.117-22.

Agarwal, O.P., 'Care and Preservation of Museum Objects', NRLCP, Lucknow (1977).

Sengupta, Arputharani, 'Conservation of Decorative Textile' Conservation of Cultural Property in India, Vol. XXXII & XXXIII (1999-2000), pp.53-57.

Gulati, A.N., 'The Patolu of Gujarat', Museums Association Of India (1951). Encyclopedia Britannica, Vol. 22 (1947), p. 5.

Stack, Lotus, 'Patterned Threads Ikat Traditions and Inspirations' Exhibition catalogue held at The Minneapolis Institute of Arts, Minneapolis, U.S.A., 27th June-6th September, 1987, pp.12-15.

Stack, Lotus, 'The Essential Threads Tapestry on Wall and Body', Exhibition Catalogue held at The Minneapolis Institute of Arts, Minneapolis, U.S.A., 25th June–2nd October 1988, pp.12-15.

Bhatnagar , I.K., 'Brocaded Textiles and Their Conservation', Conservation of Cultural Property In India, Vol.8 (1975), pp.41-45. and Vol.11 (1978), pp. 73-75.

Watt, Sir George, 'Indian Art at Delhi,1903', Government Printing Press, India, pp. 360-417.

Agarwala, V.S., 'Harsacharita - Ek Samskriti ka Adhyayana', 1953 (Hindi).

Peters, R.H., 'Early dyeing theories and dyeing theories based on the latest research data,' CIBA Rev., (1964) No.2, pp. 2-29.

Timar-Balazsy, Agnes & Eastop, Dinah, 'Chemical Principles of Textile Conservation', Oxford: Butterworth-Heinemann (2005).

Choudhuri, B.K., Banerjee, R.K & Sanyal, B. K., 'Removal of tarnish from gold saris and embroideries,' Research and Industry, Delhi, (1963), pp. 70-71. Delft Conference on conservation of textiles', 1964, preprints, IIC, London, 2nd edition 1965, p. 153.

Morley, Grace, 'Museum collection in India Pre-Columbian Art as a New-Note;' Journal of Indian Museums, Museums Association of India, Vol. XXI-XXIV (1965-68), PP.19-26.

Gulati,A.N., 'Patolu of Gujarat' published by the Museums Association of India (1951)

Thomson, Garry, 'The Museum Environment', an IIC publicaion, Butterworths, London (1978)

Vargas, J. C., 'Reinforcing treatment of silk embroidery threads with carboxy methyl chitosan and chitosan acetate', Poster presented at the 14th Triennial Meeting The Hague ,12th-16th September 2005,ICOM Committee For Conservation, Preprints Volume II, pp.997-1000.

Sousa, Micaela & Melo, Maria Joao, 'A 'green' approach to antique textile cleaning', Preprints of the 14th Triennial Meeting The Hague, 12th-16th September 2005, ICOM Committee For Conservation, Vol II, pp.944-953.

Vander Wateren,K., '2000 The Karwatti Method, even the restorer goes digital.' In Jaarbek 2000,Textile Conservation: past, present, future. Stiching Textilcommissie, Nederland.

J.Vuori, & N. Britton, 'A preliminary investigation of digital inkjet printing on sheer fabrics for textile conservation,' 15th Triennial Conference, New Delhi, 22-26 Sept. 2008.

Chandra, Moti, 'Costumes, textiles, cosmetics and coiffure in ancient and mediaeval India,' 1973, Oriental, Delhi, pp.188.

Caple, Chris, 'Conservation skills - Judgment' Method and Decision making?, Routledee, London.

Chandra, Moti, 'Ancient Indian ivories',. Bulletin of the Prince of Wales Museum, No.6, 1957-59, pp.4-63.

Chandra, Moti, 'An Ivory Figyre from Ter', Lalit Kala Vol.8 (1960), pp. 7-14.

Davidson, J.L., 'Begram Ivories and Early Indian Sculpture-A Reconsideration of Date', P.Pal (ed.), Aspects of Indian Art-Papers presented in a Symposium at Los Angeles County Museum of art, October 1970, Leiden (1972), pp, 1-14.

Dwivedi, V.P., 'A pair of ivory figures from Orissa'. Oriental Art. 13, 1967. pp 94-97.

Idib., 'Indian Ivories', Agam Kala Prakashan, Delhi (1976).

Idib., 'Ivories Indiens,' Arts Asiatiques, Vol. 16 (1967), pp. 59-74.

Idib., 'Kashmir Ivory carvings' Chhavi (Bharat Kala Bhavan Golden Jubilee Volume), Varanasi, 1972.

Espinoza, E.O., 'Identification Guide for Ivory and Ivory Substitutes' 2nd ed., The World Wildlife Fund, 1992

Graven, H., 'Fragments of a portable altar from Siegburg in the Kestner Museum, Hannover.' *Jahrhuch der Koniglich preussischen Kunstsammlungen* 21; 1900, pp. 75-98, (German).

Jones, M., 'Fake?-The art of deception'. 1990, British Museum Publications, London.

Kruger, F. Johan, 'The use of divisible isotopic and chemical labels to control the world ivory trad', S. African Journal Wildlife Research. 26/4, (1996) pp.131-132.

Plenderleith, H.J., 'The conservation of antiquities and works of art: Treatment, Repair and Restoration', 1956, Oxford University Press, London.

Forschungslabor, 'Authenticity-testing at the Rathgen Research Laboratory.' Kunst und Faelschung. (1979), pp. 24-32, [German].

Shell, Harvey, Is It Ivory?, Ahio, 1983

Trench, Lucy, ed. 'Materials and techniques in the decorative arts: An illustrated dictionary', Chicago, University of Chicago Press; 2000.

Loss, M.C. 'A Gothic ivorv mirror-case', *The Journal of the Walters Art Gallery* 2: 1939. pp. 109.

Uniclectica Antiques and Collectables Online Series: Caring for your Antiques and Collectibles.

Wills, Geoffrey Ivory. ?, AS Barnes; 1969.

Web site of 'Chicago Appraisers Association' http://www.chicagoappraisers.com/ivory-carvings.html

Agrawala, R.C., 'Early Indian Bone Figures in the National Museum, New Delhi', East and West, 1968, 18, nos. 3-4, pp. 311-314.

Auboyer, J., 'Private Life in Ancient India as seen from the ivory Sculptures of Begram', Marg, XXIV, 3, 1971, pp. 47-54.

Barrett, D., 'Ter', The Heritage of Indian Art,' Bombay (1960), 5, pp.8-9.

Idib., 'Ancient Indian Ivories', Bulletin of the Prince of Wales Museum of Western India, 6, 1957-59, pp. 4-63.

Chandra, Moti 'An Ivory Figure from Ter,' Lalit Kala, 8, 1960, pp. 7-14.

Deshpande, M.N., 'Some Observations on the Ivory Figure from Ter', Lalit Kala, 1961, 10, pp.55-56.

D'Ancona, M.L., 'An Indian Statuette from Pompeii' Artibus Asiae 1950, XVII, pp.166-180.

Maiuri, A., 'The Ivory Statuette of Indian Art at Pompeii,' Journal of U.P. Historic Society XIX, 1946, pp.1-9.

Mehendale, S., 'The Ivory Statuette from Bhokardan and its connection to Ivory Statuettes from Pompaeii and Ter,' South Asian Archaeology 1991, Stuttgart 1993, pp. 529-538.

Sivaramamurti, C., 'Begram Ivories: The Tradition of the Master Craftsman', Marg XXI, 3 (1971), pp.9-14.

Cristoferi, E. & Fiori, C, 'Polishing Treatment on ivory material in the National Museum in Ravenna,' Studies in Conservation, Vol. 37, no.4 (1992), pp. 259-266.

Godfrey, L.M., Ghisalberti, E.L., Beng, E.W., Byrne, L.T. & Richardson, G.W., 'The Analysis of Ivory from a Marine Environment', Studies in Conservation, Vol. 47, No.1 (2002), pp. 29-45.

Freund, Anke, Eggert, Gerhard, Kutzke, Hartmut & Barbier, Bruno, 'On occurrence of magnesium phosphates on ivory', Studies in Conservation, Vol.47, No. 3 (2002), pp. 155-160.

Kalbeek, Nicoline & Richter, Jane, 'Preservation of Burned Bones: An Investigation of the Effects of Temperature and pH on Hardness,' Studies in Conservation, Vol.51, No.2 (2006), pp. 123-138.

Child, A.M., 'Microbial taphonomy of archaeological bone', Studies in Conservation, Vol.40, No.1 (1995), pp.19-30.

Bunn, Maureen, 'Saran as a treatment for bone', Book, U.K. Institute for Conservation, on Archaeological bone, antler and ivory, (1987), pp.28-33.

Cherfas, Jeremy, 'Science gives ivory a sense of identity', Science, 246, no. 4934, pp.1120-1221.

Ellam, Diane, 'Wet bone: the potential for freeze-drying', Book, U.K. Institute for Conservation, on Archaeological bone, antler and ivory, (1987), pp.34-35.

Matienzo, L.J. & Snow, C.E., 'The chemical effect of hydrochloric acid and organic solvents on the surface of ivory', Studies in Conservation, Vol. 31 (1986), pp. 133-139.

Lafontaine, R.H., & Wood, P.A., 'The Stabilization of Ivory Against Relative Humidity Fluctuations', Studies in Conservation, Vol. 27 (1982), pp. 109-117.

Agrawal, O.P., 'Care and Preservation of Museum objects', NLRCP, Lucknow, India (1977), pp. 107.

Baer, N.S., Indictor, N., Frantz, J.H. & Appelbaum, B., 'The effect of high temperature on Ivory', Studies in Conservation, Vol.16 (1971), pp.1-8. Science for Conservators, volume 3, p. 123.

Rosa Maria Cimino, Ancient Rome and India, "Commercial and cultural contacts between the Roman World and

India," Munshiram Manoharlal Publishers Pvt. Ltd., New Delhi

Radley, J. A., & Grant, J., 'Fluorescence analysis in Ultraviolet light' Chayman and Hall, London (1959).

Muller, G.C.W., 'The book of Ivory,' London (1938).

Penniman, T .K., 'Pictures of Ivory and other Animal Teeth, Bone and Antler', Pitt Rivers Museum, Oxford (1952).

Maskell, A .O., 'Ivory in commerce and in the arts,' Journal of the Royal society of arts (1960), Vol. 54.

Dwivedi, V.P., 'Ivory and Bone carvings in the National Museum Collections,' bulletin, National Museum, New Delhi, No.2 (1970), pp.29-31.

Ibid., 'Ancient Indian Ivories-A fresh study' Archaeological Congress and Seminar papers (ed.) S.B. Deo; Nagpur, 1972), pp. 245-250.

Ibid., 'Ivories of North-west India,'Aspects of Indian Art,(ed. P.Pal, E.J. Brill, Leiden, 1973).

Ibid., 'Ancient Indian Ivory Carvings 'Smt Indira Gandhi Felicitation Volume' Allahabad.

Ibid., 'Ivory carvings as a source of ancient Art history, Heritage of India (L.N. Mishra Commemoration Volume), 1978.

Lal Krishna, 'New Gallery: Decorative Arts', Journal of Indian Museums, Museums Association of India, Vol. XLVII (1991), pp.113-115.

Dwivedi, V.P., 'An Ivory comb from Orissa', Journal of Indian Museums, Museums Association of India, Vol. XXX-XXXI (1974-75), pp. 72-74.

Kuhn, Herman, 'The Conservation and Restoration of Works of Art and Antiquities', Vol. 1 (1987), Butterworths-Heinlmann, London.

Stolow, Nathan, 'Conservation and Exhibition', 1987, Butterworths, London.

Basham, A.L., 'The wonder that was India', pp. 207-210.

Rig Veda, Tr. G.R. Nandargikar, Delhi, 1890.10, XXXIV, 5.

Ramayana, Oriental Institute, Baroda (1960).

Ibid., Ayodhyakanda, 69, 12.

Ibid., Sundrakanda, 10, 2.

Ibid., Sundrakanda, 9, 22-23.

Ibid., Aranyakanda, 55, 8.

Ibid., Kiskindakanda, 38, 12.

Chandra, Moti, 'Nidhisringa (Cornucopia); A study in Symbolism,' Bulletin of the Prince of Wales Museum, no.9, p.10.

Agarwal,V.S., 'Kadambari-Ek sanskrita Adhayana',Varanashi, 1970, p.49.

Agarwal, D.P., 'Harappan chronology: are - examination of the evidence', Studies in Prehistory, pp. 139-148.

Pal, M.K. , 'Ivory Works in India through the Ages', New Delhi, 1972, p.14.

Mackay, E., 'Early Indus Civilization', London (1948), p.131.

Ibid., 'Further Excavations at Mohenjo-daro, (2 Vols.) Vol. 1, p. 117.

Rao, S.R., 'The Excavations at Lothal', Lalit kala, No.3-4, p.87.

Ibid., 'Further Excavations at Lothal' Lalit kala, No.11 (April, 1962), p. 23.

Lal, B.B. & Thapar, B. K., 'Excavations at Kalibangan' Cultural Forum, IX, No.4, p.80.

Marshall John, 'Mohenjo-daro and the Indus Civilization,' (3 vols.) London 1931.

Agarwala, R.C., 'Early Indian bone figures in the National Museum, New Delhi, East West, (N.S.) Vol. 18, Nos. 3-4, Rome, 1968, pp. 311-314.

Auboyer, Jeannine, 'Ancient Indian Ivories from Begram, Afghanistan,' Journal of the Indian Society of Oriental Art, XVI, (1948), pp. 34-46.

Asher, F.M., 'Buddhist ivories from Kashmir,' O.A., XVIII, No. 4, pp.367-373.

Beach, Milo C., 'Two Indian Ivories; newly acquired,' Bulletin of the Museum of fine arts, Vol. LXI I, No. 329, Boston, 1964, pp. 95-101.

Bhattacharya, A.K., 'A survey of the art and techniques of ivory in India', Studies in Indian Culture, (Dr. Ghulam Yazdani commemoration volume) Hydrabad, 1966, pp. 137-144.

Deshpand, M.N., 'Some observation on ivory figure from Ter', Lalit Kala, No.10, New Delhi, 1962, pp.55-56.

Ghosh, Ajit, 'Some old Indian Ivories', Rupam, No.32,Calcutta, Oct. 1927, pp.122-129.

Jayaswal, K.P., 'An Early Ivory', Journal of the Indian Society of Oriental Art, Vol. IV, No.1, June 1936, p.75.

Moti chandra, 'Some old ivories from Orissa', Puspanjali, Vol.1, No.1, Bombay 1963, pp.3739.

Nandi, Sipra, 'Art of ivory in Murshidabad', Indian Museum Bulletin, Vol. IV, No.1, pp.93-99.

Nanavati, J.M., 'Ivory figurines from Prabhasa', Journal of the M.P. *Itihasa* Parishad, No.4, Bhopal, pp.57-61.

Sivaramamurti, C., 'Begram Ivories: the tradition of the master craftsman', Marg XXIV, No.2, Bombay, pp.9-14.

Vogel J. Ph., 'Note on an Ivory statutte from Pompeii', Annual Bibliography of Indian Archaeology, Vol. XI1, 1938, Leyden, 1 949, pp. 1-5.

Josef Riederer, 'Restoration & Preservation', An Exibition of Modern Techniques of Restoration for the Preservation of Cultural Property, Goethe-Institute, Munich (1989), pp. 76-77.

Gairola,T.R., 'Restoration and Preservation of Archaeological Museum Exibits (Ivory, Bone and Horn)', The Journal of Indian Museums (MAI), Vol.V (1949), p. 35.

Agrawal, V.S., 'Inter-Asian Exhofibition of Art and Archaeology', The Journal of Indian Museums (MAI),Vol.III (1947), pp.29-35.

Varma, D.N., 'A New Ivory Gallery in The Salar Jung Museum, Hyderabad,' Journal of Indian Museums (MAI), Vol. XXXIX (1983), pp.166-168.

Satya Prakash, 'A note on the manufacture of Rajasthan Bracelets', The Journal of Indian Museums (MAI), Vol X (1954), p. 36.

Dupree, Nancy Hatch, Dupree Louis & Motamedi, A.A., 'The National Museum of Afghanistan An Illustrated Guide' Kabul, 1974.

Plenderlieth, H.J., & Werner, A.E.A., 'The Conservation of Antiquities and Works of Art,' (2nd. Ed.) London, Oxford University Press, 1971.

C. Pearson (ed.), 'Conservation of Wet Organic Artifacts Excluding Wood. In *Conservation of Marine Archaeological Objects*,' Butterworths, London, 1987, pp. 122-163.

Thomson, G.(ed.), *'Recent Advances in Conservation,'* Butterworths, London,1963.

Lafontaine, R. H., & P. A. Wood., 'The Stabilization of Ivory Against Relative Humidity Fluctuations,' *Studies in Conservation, 27* (1982), pp. 109-117.

Matienzo, L. J., & C. E. Snow, The Chemical Effects of Hydrochloric Acid and Organic Solvents on the Surface of Ivory. *Studies in Conservation,* 31 (1986), pp. 133-139.

Werner, A.E.A., The Conservation of leather, wood, bone and ivory, and archival materials, *The Conservation of Cultural Property,* Museum and Monuments XI (1968), pp. 237-249. UNESCO, Paris.

UNESCO, 'Synthetic material used in the conservation of cultural material.', *The Conservation of Cultural Property with Special Reference to Tropical Conditions.*

Museum and Monuments Series XI, (1968), pp. 303-331, Paris.

Rosa Mario Cimino, Science For Conservators 'Introduction to Materials', *Vol. 1, The Conservation Unit, Conservation Science Teaching Series, Science For Conservators, Cleaning, Vol. 2, Museums and Galleries, Conservation Science Teaching Series, Science For Conservators, Adhesives and Coatings, Vol. 3, Cconservation Science Teaching Series Museums and Galleries CommissionÑ* London., (1992),

Bisht, A.S., 'Science in the aid of detection of fakes with special reference to Ivories - a case study,' *Conservation of cultural property in India,* vol. 22, 1989, pp. 31-35

Melwani, Lavino, 'OBJET D'ART-Art Shine',Swagat A Media Transasia publication for Air India, September 2007, pp.70-81.

Chatterjee, J.K., 'Precision, Beauty and Art, A Tradition in Ivory', The Week, March 13-18, 1988, pp. 32-33.

# INDEX

## C

## D

# E

# F

## G



## H

## I

## J

## K



## L

**M**

## N

## O

## P

## Q



## R



## S

## T

## U

**X**



**Y**



**Z**